Advancing Women
in Business—
The Catalyst Guide

Catalyst

Foreword by Sheila W. Wellington,
President, Catalyst

Advancing Women in Business— The Catalyst Guide

Best Practices from the Corporate Leaders

Jossey-Bass Publishers
San Francisco

Substantial discounts on bulk quantities of Jossey-Bass books are available to corporations, professional associations, and other organizations. For details and discount information, contact the special sales department at Jossey-Bass Inc., Publishers (415) 433-1740; Fax (800) 605-2665.

For sales outside the United States, please contact your local Simon & Schuster International Office.

www.josseybass.com

Manufactured in the United States of America on Lyons Falls Turin Book. This paper is acid-free and 100 percent totally chlorine-free.

Library of Congress Cataloging-in-Publication Data

Advancing women in business—the Catalyst guide : best practices from the corporate leaders / foreword by Sheila Wellington. — 1st ed.
    p. cm. — (The Jossey-Bass business & management series)
    Includes index.
    ISBN 0–7879–3966–8 (acid-free paper)
    1. Businesswomen. 2. Career development. I. Catalyst, inc.
II. Series.
HD6053.A38 1998
650.1—dc21   97–45394

FIRST EDITION
HB Printing   10 9 8 7 6 5 4 3 2 1

The Jossey-Bass
Business & Management Series

Contents

Foreword

Sheila W. Wellington

We at Catalyst work with business and the professions to enable women in business to achieve their maximum potential and to assist employers in capitalizing on the talents of women. Whether the issue is women's advancement, turnover, or work-family balance, Catalyst finds research-driven, practical, workable solutions to the gender challenge faced by corporations and professional firms. A business imperative, tapping women's talent has moved to the priority list of the business leaders who understand that by 2005, women will make up 47 percent of the U.S. workforce.

Catalyst partners with U.S. corporations and professional firms that understand the critical power of women at work, that know that women's advancement is not a feel-good or even a do-good issue but a bottom-line practicality. For three decades, we have studied work environments, human resource policies, and employment practices to identify those that effectively advance women to senior management positions. Our research identifies barriers and opportunities for women, providing practical how-to guidance to companies committed to promoting gender diversity. We combine our extensive knowledge base with real-world advisory experience helping major corporations and professional firms create tailored, workable change programs. Our objective is lasting, measurable results.

The Catalyst Award honors the innovative approaches companies take to address women's recruitment, development, and advancement.

In giving these awards, Catalyst provides the business community with proven success models so that other corporations and professional firms can conceive initiatives that are good for women and good for business.

It is in this spirit that Catalyst publishes our first edition of model initiatives and practices, *Advancing Women in Business—The Catalyst Guide: Best Practices from the Corporate Leaders*. Some of the best practices that we include here have won the Catalyst Award; others are stellar aspects of initiatives-in-progress; still others we know from our work inside corporations and firms.

This collection reflects current practices and is not meant to be exhaustive, but rather representative of programs and practices that have been proved to work at many of the nation's most successful and profitable corporations and firms. These are the ones worth emulating. From these, others will germinate; we will watch them as they raise the bar, and we look forward to publishing the sequel.

We present these best practices as possibilities. But let me season Catalyst's counsel with a caveat: best practices for gender diversity cannot be dropped into an organization and expected to dissolve problems magically. Companies and firms must avoid the common temptation to leap at solutions, diversity structures, and training before diversity is secured as part of the organization's overall business plan and the real issues have been identified and understood.

Catalyst recommends that change be approached systemically. The diversity challenge faced by businesses today results from corporate structures and systems established yesterday, in a time prior to women's full-scale entrance into the workforce. Across many industries and in many professional firms, gender diversity initiatives have been disadvantaged by the permanence of a culture where a structured and rigid environment reinforces out-of-date behaviors. Diverse workers face challenges to advancing in environments not accustomed to incorporating difference.

More and more smart companies now understand the importance of using the widest range of talent available. These companies and firms are focusing on a soup-to-nuts approach, ranging from hiring and recruitment to career pathing and mentoring, all based solidly on commitment from top leadership and on fixing accountability for making change happen.

We hope that the best practices included here will serve as catalysts for other corporations and firms, who will take the measure of what is appropriate and resize them for individual fit. We offer these practices as guidelines and benchmarks for those who know the time has come to join the corporate leaders.

Acknowledgments

This book was conceived by Catalyst President Sheila W. Wellington along with Cedric Crocker of Jossey-Bass, an enlightened editor who understands the importance to Catalyst's mission of disseminating the information that resides in our files and in the heads of our experts.

Thanks go to all the staff at Catalyst, whose accumulated knowledge has made this book possible. Thanks in particular to Betty Spence, whose knowledge, skills, and passion for this project literally made it happen. Thanks also to Barbara Presley Noble for her keen reportorial and writing contributions on the project. We acknowledge Mary Mattis, both for her perspective on the project and for her remarkable insights on benchmarking. Jo Weiss afforded a critical addition to the Catalyst approach to working with companies and firms, and Marcia Kropf and Bickley Townsend helped formulate the book's scope. Julia Resnick contributed her insight from initial plan through final research. Thanks to Dawn Fisher for her interview assistance. Special thanks go to Carrie Lane for rapid turnaround of critical research details and verification of data, and to her and David Petitt for assistance with corporate liaison, including interviews.

We are grateful to all the companies and firms whose best practices appear here, not least of all because they are leaders in women's advancement. We thank in particular the individuals at those organizations who took the time to be interviewed and verify information.

We give special thanks to the chief executives whose candid interviews reveal their motivations for advancing women and show not only that it can be done but how it can be done.

Introduction

- In 1986, Motorola initiated a companywide parity initiative requiring that in ten years, the representation of women and people of color at every management level correspond to those qualified in these groups in the general population. The Organization and Management Development Review reaches down to the entry and middle levels of management and holds these managers accountable for developing and retaining women and people of color.

- The Bank of Montreal instituted a corporate strategy makeover in the early 1990s, to which bank executives attribute its subsequent four years of record profits. A critical component of the new strategy was a workplace equality initiative designed to attract and maximize the potential of women in the organization.

- In the late 1980s, Morrison & Foerster, a San Francisco–based law firm, began losing its mid- and senior-level associates, especially the women among them, at an alarming—and costly—rate. The new generation of lawyers, it seemed, wanted time for a private life and was willing to step off the fast track to get it. MoFo stopped the talent drain by developing alternatives to the traditional model of law firm success. It made work-life quality a central component of the firm's culture.

- When a group of female engineers at Hewlett-Packard decided that the few women at the company needed to know more about each other and their technical contributions, they formed the

Technical Women's Conference. With the company's blessing, they organized a yearly conference that turned into a major networking-information, career-advice, leadership-training event; last year, they held three regional conferences instead of one huge one; all told, thirty-five hundred women attended.

These initiatives are not simply targeted at women. They represent a new way of thinking about competitiveness at these leading-edge organizations and others that will be described in the course of this volume. The leaders of these companies have realized that competitive advantage derives less and less from manufacturing processes, low costs, or even innovative products. In the next few decades, a company will compete increasingly on the quality of its workforce. Human capital—the creativity, analytical skills, and leadership ability of employees—will be the competitive advantage. To become successful and grow, companies must attract the most talented employees. In every industry, one of the most important new organizational goals will be for companies to turn themselves into magnets for women.

Accordingly, companies must look to expand beyond the traditional white-male pools of talent to new sources. As a senior vice president of a Catalyst Award–winning company told Catalyst, "Those companies that prosper in the nineties will, other things being equal, be those that draw upon the largest pool of trained ability. More and more, that will mean recruiting women, who represent a steadily increasing proportion of the trained labor force."

Demographics support that contention. Women are already an important presence in the workforce:

- Forty-six percent of the total workforce now is female, according to 1996 Bureau of Labor Statistics figures. More than half of all women work full-time outside the home.

- Women now earn more than half the bachelor's and master's degrees awarded every year, according to the

U.S. Department of Education 1996 *Digest of Education Statistics*.

- Women earn one-third of the MBAs, according to the U.S. Department of Education 1996 *Digest of Education Statistics*. In addition, virtually half of all new business, law, and doctoral degrees decorate the office walls of women, and half of the undergraduate degrees in business and management, accounting, and mathematics go to women as well.

Companies are also learning that a focus on women can both add value and reduce costs:

Consumer impact: Service- and product-oriented businesses are increasingly aware that women are often the primary decision makers on a range of consumer purchases. Women make more than 85 percent of total household purchasing decisions, including such major areas as homes, cars, vacations, and home improvement. The organization of the future, many executives argue, needs people at all levels who reflect the demographics of the consumer base—and such individuals are especially needed in senior positions, providing leadership.

Cost reduction: Many organizations have been successful in increasing the number of women in entry-level management positions, but less successful at developing their talent and making certain they stay in the pipeline to the upper levels of the organization. Companies and firms lose the significant investment they make in the early careers of individuals who leave. Turnover costs of exempt employees have been estimated as between 90 percent and 150 percent of annual salary. Yet a recent Catalyst survey indicates that many companies have not yet placed the development of female capital high on their strategic priority lists. We want this book to change that.

Exhibit I.1. Capitalizing on Women as a Resource

A strong, multifaceted business rationale underlies the impetus to develop fully the talents of women.

Economic Drivers:

Illustrative

Changing Global Environment

- Changing workforce demographics
- Top talent cuts across demographic groups
- Competition for scarce resources
- Globalization of business
- Women drive 85%+ of purchase decisions
- Women emerging as decision makers among customers and competitors

Opportunities from Capitalizing on Diversity

Develop team and decision-making skills to full potential

- Diverse perspectives generate wider range of issues and solutions

Maximize marketing efforts to women and minority customers and clients

- Workforce mirroring customer base improves appeal, customer service, retention, innovation

Higher quality workforce from tapping top talent across demographic groups

Maximize employee commitment

Costs of Failure to Meet Diverse Workforce Needs

Undesired turnover

- Loss of talent to competitors or entrepreneurial start-ups
- Loss of investment in training
- Loss of value of experience
- Learning curve costs for replacement

Sub-par recruiting results

Productivity loss from low morale, unsupportive environment (men and women), absenteeism

Opportunity costs of failing to capitalize on diversity (e.g., implications for marketing, team/decision-making skills, workforce quality, commitment, shareholder/stakeholder dissatisfaction)

Barriers to Retaining and Advancing Women

Because of the gains made in education, women have achieved virtual parity with men when entering corporations, firms, and other organizations. Yet research shows that within five or six years, women begin to drop off the fast track. By the start of what should be the mid-game of a high-powered career, many women disappear. Some women, no doubt, simply execute their "right of exit," as economists say, but Catalyst has found in its years of studying organizational dynamics that more often companies, wittingly and unwittingly, create conditions that disadvantage women. Catalyst has identified the following as the most powerful barriers to female career advancement:

- Negative assumptions in executive ranks about women, their abilities, and their commitment to careers

- Perceptions that women don't fit with the corporate culture

- Lack of career planning and the range of job experiences commensurate with the future needs of the organization

- Lack of core opportunities for female employees who have management potential

- Assumption that women will not relocate for career advancement

- Failure to make managers accountable for advancing women

- Management reluctance to giving women line (that is, revenue-generating) experience

- Absence of, or too limited, succession planning

- "Negative mentoring" and self-selection where women move into staff areas instead of line positions

- Lack of mentoring and exclusion from informal career networks, where men have typically learned the unwritten rules of success

- Appraisal and compensation systems that are not uniform for men and women

- Corporate systems designed prior to women's large-scale infusion into the workplace, such as benefits systems and productivity measures that don't take into account new policies such as flexible work arrangements

- Other forms of "cultural discouragement," like a work environment that values long hours over actual performance or that offers limited support for work-family initiatives and limited commitment to diversity programs in general

- Discrimination and sexual harassment

Who This Book Is For

Advancing Women in Business—The Catalyst Guide: Best Practices from the Corporate Leaders is aimed broadly at companies and firms contemplating initiatives for women's advancement. It will provide a set of principles and practical methods developed by Catalyst for retaining and advancing women in corporations and firms. It will be useful to the following:

- Corporate and firm leaders and other high-level people who intend to champion diversity and other new forms of work organization at their companies. Catalyst believes the ability of a company's leadership to articulate how its vision of gender diversity fits in with overall business goals is critical to an initiative's success.

Figure I.1. What Holds Women Back From Advancement?

Ranked in order
of Female
Executive Responses

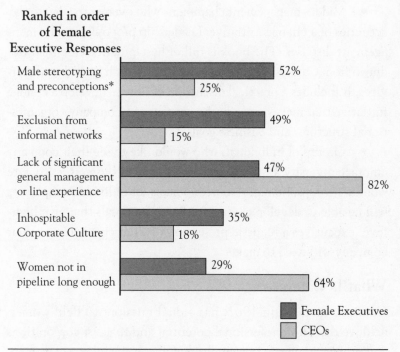

Note: Stereotypes and preconceptions include
- Not committed to careers
- Not willing to work long hours
- Not aggressive enough or too aggressive
- Will not relocate
- Lack proper training or skills

Source: Catalyst research: *Women in Corporate Leadership* (1996); *Cracking the Glass Ceiling: Strategies for Success* (1994).

This book includes the voices of chief executives and other corporate and professional leaders.

• Middle-management champions who oversee the day-to-day activities of a change initiative. Leadership proposes, middle management disposes. The book is full of best-practice case histories drawn from Catalyst's long experience in research and advisory services. It includes a practical discussion of how to develop a change initiative that makes sense in the context of a company's organizational structures and business goals.

• Groups of individuals who would like to see their company embrace diversity. Using *Advancing Women in Business*, corporate women's groups, human resources officers, or individual employees will be able to develop change initiative proposals that give high-level executives a realistic projection of what commitment their company will need to make.

What Is Catalyst?

Catalyst, founded in 1962, has a dual mission: to help women achieve their full professional potential and to assist corporations and professional firms in capitalizing fully on the talents of women. Catalyst conducts original research; offers advisory services to corporations and professional firms on the recruitment, retention, and advancement of women; and works with corporations to identify women for their boards of directors. We are well known to the public for giving out the Catalyst Award, an annual recognition of companies with particularly innovative or creative approaches to advancing and retaining women.

Catalyst's Advisory Services follows these three principles:

• We bring objectivity and a broad-based understanding of the many issues surrounding women's advancement in the workplace.

• We work collaboratively with our clients to understand their unique needs and to create tailored, practical solutions.

- We focus on having long-term, measurable impact within the companies we serve.

We have worked with a diverse client base, including manufacturing, consumer, health care, retail, and financial organizations, as well as law, consulting, and accounting firms. We have found that though organizations may be structured very differently, there tends to be common ground across structural types. Similar issues arise again and again, no matter what the structural context. We offer an approach that addresses the unique structural issues within a professional services firm versus a corporation, for example, but also speaks to the issues most organizations share when creating a change initiative with a component promoting women's advancement.

What Are Best Practices?

Catalyst uses the term *best practices* to describe the building blocks of initiatives. In theoretical terms, a best practice is a context-specific solution to a problem or barrier. In practical terms, a best practice is a component of a change initiative that, when linked up with other best practices, will allow the organization to arrive at its larger long-term goals. They share the following characteristics:

- Best practices don't exist in isolation or out of context. Although the overall retention and development issues may not change markedly from one company to another or one industry to another, problem-solving methods may. What works in one company or industry may not work in another.

- Best practices evolve and change. What worked three, four, or five years ago may not work now.

- Best practices may be shaped by several factors: industry, company size, organizational structure (for example, company versus firm), workforce composition.

- Implementing best practices may not follow a totally predictable course. It is normal for unexpected consequences to arise. Organizations need to plan to adapt and expand practices as they are implemented.

Source Material

This book brings together the different threads of Catalyst's expertise to reach the widest possible audience. Three types of material serve as sources: Catalyst research reports, case histories from our advisory services work, and best practices from winners of the Catalyst Award.

Catalyst research reports: Catalyst, one of the first organizations to look into the phenomenon now widely known as the *glass ceiling,* has delivered major reports on a range of topics, including parental leave policies (1992), women in corporate leadership (1996), women's career advancement (1992), work flexibility (1997, 1996), building effective corporate women's groups (1988), women in sales (1995), and women in engineering (1994). The 1998 research report schedule includes the following topics: women of color in corporate America, dual-career couples, and women entrepreneurs. Each of these reports contains information companies need to make a case for change initiatives, as well as examples of what has and hasn't worked in different types of organizations.

Case histories: Catalyst undertakes a variety of customized, in-company research and advisory assignments on a proprietary basis. Catalyst is often invited into an organization to assess, assist, or troubleshoot. In our confidential reports to those companies, we evaluate the organization's goals and environment, recommend strategies that will advance women in the organization, and provide examples of practices that have worked in similar situations in different companies.

Catalyst has conducted internal studies for numerous top industrial and manufacturing organizations, including leading chemical companies, an industrial foods corporation, an international manufacturer of heavy equipment, and a major automobile manufacturer. We have studied and provided guidance on the environment for women at plant sites, research and development facilities, field locations, and corporate headquarters, both in the United States and overseas. Catalyst has also conducted studies with client-driven professional services firms, including a major public accounting firm, leading national law firms, and financial services firms. In addition, we provide advisory counsel to accounting and management consulting firms.

Catalyst Award recipients: In 1997, we celebrated the tenth anniversary of the Catalyst Award, which recognizes companies and organizations that have successful initiatives to advance women. Initiatives undergo extensive scrutiny, including three-day site visits, and winners are notable for their link to business rationale, accountability, and the support of senior management and the corporate culture. The four companies highlighted at the opening of this Introduction are recent winners, along with Allstate, Avon Mexico, Deloitte & Touche, Dow Chemical Company, Hoechst Celanese Corporation, J.C. Penney Company, Knight-Ridder, McDonald's, and Texas Instruments.

The Catalyst Information Center serves as a repository of corporate best practices for building gender diversity and as a national clearinghouse for information on women and work. With access to the most current materials and statistics on women's workplace issues, Catalyst information specialists monitor developments and respond daily to requests in more than two hundred subject areas, from women in the financial industry to alternative work schedules and mentoring.

Another major resource at Catalyst is the expertise of its research staff, which has done groundbreaking work in organizational dynamics and the impact of gender on employment opportunity. They have interviewed hundreds of executives of companies and firms, conducted employee surveys and focus groups, and developed the contextual approach that Catalyst finds the most effective way to advocate for change.

How to Use This Book

We assume our readers will be looking for inspiration and practical advice on developing change initiatives that will help retain their most valuable employees, women or men.

Advancing Women in Business offers an antidote for what happens to many women entering the middle years of their careers: they slow down, get derailed, disappear, or opt out of competition for advancement. The book includes a comprehensive introduction to the Catalyst approach to organizational change, offers case studies of corporate change initiatives, and provides examples of best practices in such areas as leadership, career development, flexible work arrangements, succession planning, and sexual harassment prevention.

Readers will be able to use *Advancing Women in Business* to develop their own long-term change initiatives or to think creatively about what best practices fit most appropriately with their own organizational strategies.

Finally, readers will benefit from the experiences of people involved in the day-to-day management of change initiatives. Leading companies are on the cusp of the second generation of diversity initiatives, beginning to think of creative ways to keep the momentum of initiatives started in the early 1990s. *Advancing Women in Business* will help interested organizations look to the future as well as to the present.

Part I

Changing the System

The Catalyst Approach

Catalyst has found that efforts to maximize the value of a workforce by capitalizing on the talents of women are likely to be successful only when an organization takes an inclusive, problem-solving, comprehensive approach. Short-term, quick-win approaches to developing the talent of women can be used in kicking off an initiative, but if there is no follow-through and no competitive strategy, the initiative is unlikely to have great impact in the long term. Career development in general should take place in the context of an organization (more harmonious cultural dynamics and increased profitability, for example) and of the individual (greater opportunities, heightened job flexibility, and so on).

Creating real change for women—change that well might affect the economic results of an organization—is difficult and cannot be achieved by implementing a few isolated "women's programs." The underlying issues are almost always deeply rooted in the organization's pattern, and only an initiative aiming at systematic change will enable companies to truly capitalize on the talents of women.

With systematic change clearly established as both goal and context, most successful initiatives for women move through three stages:

- Establish a strong foundation based on leadership and a clear business case.

- Build a fact base of current barriers and opportunities for women.

- Develop and implement solutions and measurement systems.

Such a three-phase, comprehensive approach offers many benefits. It is inclusive: designed to be good for the organization, not just good for women. It provides an objective and accurate description of the environment for women in the organization's own words. Its focus is on creating opportunities, not dwelling on barriers of the past. It builds consensus around real issues and diffuses emotional reactions. It encompasses concrete mechanisms to improve women's leadership development, such as more inclusive succession planning, fair performance evaluation techniques, women's networks, and mentoring. It evaluates work-family supports that are appropriate for the organization, which might include increased flexibility, telecommuting, relocation assistance, child care options, and elder care.

Every organization desiring to improve women's advancement should always take the time to collect the facts that underlie its unique situation, to lay the fundamentals of leadership, and to clearly articulate the business reasons for change; these steps are critical to success. But each organization faces an array of solutions from which to choose—new programs such as those mentioned earlier, refinements to existing programs, metrics to define success, accountability approaches, and communication strategies and techniques.

This chapter, along with the book as a whole, offers a framework for understanding this variety, including real-world examples of the solutions that leading companies have chosen. But only through a clear understanding of your company's business case and detailed, fact-based knowledge of its unique environment will the best solutions for your organization become apparent.

Exhibit 1.1. Characteristics of Successful Change Initiatives

- Motivation and rationale linked to business strategy and profitability

- Support from the highest levels of the organization

- Built-in communication plan clearly stating how the best practices are linked to business issues

- Built-in accountability mechanism so that the initiative doesn't become a management fad that employees can ignore

Launching a comprehensive initiative for women can seem daunting, but it is doable, as the examples in this book attest. To demystify the task somewhat, we outline here the key elements of a basic process and Catalyst's conceptual framework for bringing about change.

Phase I. Establish a Strong Foundation

Champions of change for women must address two fundamental questions: Why is this particular change good for the organization? Who will lead the change? Successful initiatives clearly communicate to all employees that focusing on the advancement of women is a good business strategy. The involvement is truly committed to a gender strategy.

Tie the initiative explicitly to a business rationale. Companies with employees who understand that advancing women and their strategic mission are integrated have higher success rates than those that fail to root initiatives in solid business cases. When senior executives make the business case for women's advancement, demonstrating that all employees will be beneficiaries, they give managers

Figure 1.1. Framework Based on Core Principles

Essential Element	Principle
• Committed senior management drives change	• Provide leadership vision of new culture
• Motivate and explain through business strategy rationale	• Make diversity key part of business strategy; not isolated or ad hoc
• Create specific metrics to measure results	• Create targets and flexible goals; success measures, *not* quotas
• Take long-term perspective	• Approach diversity as a systematic, ongoing process
• Build internal support through education and communication	• Focus to drive results
• Provide solid support to meet women's needs	• Address, don't ignore, manageable sources of employee stress
• Identify clear accountability	• Treat diversity goals like any other business results

tangible reasons to make a commitment to change and a way to explain it to their troops. Having a clear business case also makes it easier to defend women as a priority when other pressing issues provide the temptation to brush the effort aside. Building the business case gives companies the opportunity to refine and even extend their goals in light of the specific benefits a gender initiative will bring.

Ensure leadership support. Virtually without exception, managers involved in successful initiatives attribute success to a strong commitment from the company's top leadership. Chief executives who are open to change themselves seem most able to lead their employees through major shifts in values and practices. In such situations, the chief executive typically articulates the case for advancing women to a wide range of audiences. The company often designates an influential senior executive to champion the initiative. Several companies have developed successful initiatives by fostering alliances between employee groups and senior-level champions.

Advancing women into top positions of leadership is no small task; it involves a challenge to the way business has been done over the past decades. If CEOs and other top executives of America's corporations—overwhelmingly men—understand the facts and the potential benefits of gender equity, they will see to it that what needs to be done is done. It seems clear, however, that grassroots or unsupported efforts to advance women cannot survive in the long term on their own. When initiatives run into resistance, the support and commitment of top executives is crucial.

Phase II. Build a Fact Base

In Phase II, the company gathers information that will create the baselines for evaluating the initiative's progress. What is the current climate for women at the company? What specific barriers do they face? What is working well? What are other companies doing to attract, retain, and promote women?

Benchmark women's progress, internally and externally. A survey of current workplace demographics, including trends in hiring, turnover, and promotion, provides an objective picture of the need for targeted actions to advance women. It may pinpoint trouble spots that need particular attention and provide a baseline for evaluating progress. Finally, objective data will help efforts to prioritize the actions a company may plan to take.

Identify causes. Conducting an environmental assessment leads to an understanding of the causes—real and perceived—of barriers to women's advancement as well as of potential changes to improve women's opportunities. This typically involves some combination of focus groups, interviews, and broad-based surveys, tapping women and men at all levels of the organization as well as former company

John Bryan, Chairman and CEO, Sara Lee Corporation

John Bryan, chairman of the Sara Lee Corporation, would be the first to admit he didn't arrive at the top of the corporate heap with a feminist consciousness. He went north in 1975 to run Sara Lee after selling his Mississippi-based family business to the food giant. "I didn't have anything in my experience that included working with women in any role other than secretary or teacher." And as he points out, the idea of women in business was "undeveloped" in 1975.

But Bryan was a veteran of the civil rights movement. To support the struggle, he sent his children to the black schools in the small Mississippi town where his family was prominent, and helped build a swimming pool when local white officials closed the town pool down rather than integrate. In the late 1970s he met Felice Schwartz, the founder of Catalyst, who was making the case for women in a way that sounded familiar and logical to Bryan. "In 1980 or so I made a commencement address," he recounts. "I remember saying that women's liberation was one of the great movements beginning to take root, in the same context as blacks in America."

He joined the Catalyst board of directors and became an advocate for women's advancement. At some point, he says, he began thinking of the mix at Sara Lee, not sure that he had done all that could be done. "I asked myself, 'Are we preach-

employees. The goal of this intensive analysis, which focuses employees' perceptions and attitudes, is to unearth the underlying dynamics of differential career paths and retention rates.

Several key questions drive fact gathering, analysis, and identification of the major challenges facing women. The chart in Exhibit 1.2 on page 10 contains a sample.

ing to people but being sinners ourselves?' " In 1991, Sara Lee began doing the legwork on what would eventually become a diversity initiative particularly targeting the company's female-majority workforce.

Bryan acknowledges that his commitment to advancing and developing women is not simply social activism. Sara Lee's market is predominantly female. "I always say facetiously that I want to be identified with the cause because the company is named after a woman," he says, but there is some truth to that. Because it deals in food and garments, Sara Lee has a closer connection to its consumer base than, say, one industrial company selling ball bearings to another industrial company.

When Bryan encourages other corporate leaders to take gender diversity seriously, they sometimes retort, "It's easy for you, you sell brassieres and pantyhose," as they trot out a list of reasons for avoiding the issue. Bryan tells them they can't keep ruminating and appointing task forces. "You set some targets behind the scenes and tell people to do it," he says. "You use the same motivational techniques to promote diversity as you would to make any other choice that makes the business successful."

Yet in the next breath he says the only real barrier is a lack of conviction, suggesting there is more balance between the social activist and the corporate leader than he admits. "My convictions are strong," he says. "It's good to have convictions. It solves a lot of problems."

Phase III. Develop, Pilot, and Implement Action Plans

No initiative will be successful that is not composed of practical solutions tailored to a particular company's environment. Designers must build in both accountability and a way to measure progress.

Exhibit 1.2. Key Questions on Key Areas

Recruitment and Hiring

- What is the available talent base? How can it expand?
- What are the current strategies for the recruitment of women?
- What are the success rates?
- What key factors do women cite for their choices?

Career Development

- What role does the company play in career development?
- What elements of existing career planning practices are successful? Where is attention needed?
- How does career development differ for men and women?
- Why does the difference exist?

Advancement

- What is the typical career path to senior management or partnership?
- What differences, if any, are there in typical male and female career paths?
- What are the explicit criteria for advancement? What are the implicit criteria?
- Where in the career progression ladder do women face the greatest challenges?
- To what extent is there a glass ceiling or a set of glass walls?
- How do opportunities for women in senior management differ across business units or functional areas? Why do the differences exist?
- Are any issues related to flexibility and work-life balance?

Retention

- What are the current turnover levels for women? For men?
- At what stage in career development does turnover most frequently occur for women? For men? Why the differences?
- Why do women leave? Where do they go?

Successful action plans vary from company to company, but typically contain these tactics:

- Motivate and explain via a business rationale.

- Have committed senior managers in charge of change.

- Take a long-term perspective based on the recognition that systematic effort is usually required to make real change for women.

- Provide solid support to meet women's needs.

- Build internal support and awareness through education and communication.

- Establish clear accountability.

- Create benchmarks to gauge results.

These tactics are based on principles that reflect a practical understanding of what works and why.

Two types of targeted programs provide the infrastructure that will open up opportunities for women's advancement: leadership development and work-life supports. Many examples of practices in these areas can be found in this book.

Women's leadership development: Core human resources programs, in their design or implementation, often create unintentional barriers for women. Companies should scrutinize such areas as recruiting practices, orientation and training programs (including sexual harassment prevention), performance evaluation, benefit programs, and succession planning for evidence of differential treatment of men and women. They should revise them accordingly. In addition, leading companies have established best practices that specifically target women's career development, including mentoring, identifying high-potential women, and women's workplace networks.

Work-life supports: These programs—and the context and support provided by the organization for their success—make it possible for both women and men to balance the demands of life at work

Exhibit 1.3. The Relationship Between Principles and Basic Tactics

---

Tactic: Committed senior management drives change.

Principle: Leadership provides vision to drive systemic change.

Tactic: Motivate and explain using a business strategy rationale.

Principle: Gender diversity is a key part of doing business, not ad hoc or isolated.

Tactic: Take a long-term perspective.

Principle: Achieving real change for women is a systematic, continuing process.

Tactic: Provide solid support to meet women's needs.

Principle: Address backlash, don't ignore it.

Tactic: Build internal support and awareness through education and communication.

Principle: Focus drives results.

Tactic: Establish clear accountability.

Principle: Treat diversity goals like any other business results.

Tactic: Create benchmarks to measure progress.

Principle: Create targets and flexible goals, not quotas.

---

and life outside work. Flexible work arrangements have become more widespread in organizations in recent years, thanks to growing demand by employees and the fact that organizations benefit by being able to attract and retain valuable employees. Companies and firms recognize that a flexible environment can help them serve global customers, meet cyclical or seasonal business needs, provide continuity on projects, and deliver effective customer service. Work-

Exhibit 1.4. Aspects of a Systemic Women's Initiative

- Leadership development programs

  Identification and development of high-potential women

  Cross-functional training

  Supports that ensure women gain line experience

  Succession planning

- Mentoring programs

- Women's networks

- Work-life balance and flexibility initiatives

- Accountability

- Measuring of results

- Training

- Evaluating and modifying the initiative

---

life supports include flexible full-time options such as variations on the standard workday or workweek and telecommuting, part-time work options, leave policies, and child and elder care.

There are still hundreds of companies that have not yet made a concerted effort to change the environment of their organizations, so that women can work toward an equal role with men in corporate leadership. In many cases, this effort deficit is unintentional. The comprehensive approach described here provides opportunities for an organization on several different levels. When successful, it does what it is most directly concerned to do—it gives a company access to the widest available talent pool by helping develop strategies to recruit, retain, and advance women. In the

James Preston, Chairman and CEO, Avon Products, Inc.

Chief executives by their nature tend to be big-picture people, visionaries of the long term, so you rarely hear them talking about defining moments—those porch flashes of clarity that seem to clear the landscape of detritus.

Yet James Preston, chief executive of Avon, can take you right back to the day he "got it" about women in corporations. Not salary or employment discrimination, not sexual harassment, not the relatively tangible stuff, but the discouraging little subtextual discouragements that undermine women.

In the late 1970s, a colleague named Patricia Neighbors, the first woman to be named a vice president of Avon, worked for him, running the district sales operation. Preston says she was well ahead of her time in understanding the glass ceiling, if only because the elevation to VP came late in her career despite her talent and qualifications. Although she was a step or two below him on the corporate ladder, her experience made her a kind of mentor.

One day, without filling him in completely on her plans, Ms. Neighbors persuaded Preston to let her open a meeting of regional sales managers. She walked in, went to the podium and began greeting the assembled men. "Hello, Tom, you've changed your hairstyle, haven't you?" "Charlie, that suit looks great on you." "Jack, you're losing weight, aren't you?"

She paused, Preston says, to let the astounded silence reign for a moment, and then said, "How do you feel?" Another pause. "That's how two thousand female sales reps feel when you talk to them in such an unprofessional way."

Preston says it was a lesson in treating women professionally he didn't forget. A few years later, when corporations began to recognize the need to take special action to advance and promote women and minorities, it made sense to him viscerally. He helped institute the "Communication System for Managing Workforce Diversity."

But, as at other companies, it also made sense on a bottom-line level. "Our customer base is female, but it is also very diverse," he says. "We have large constituencies in the African American and Hispanic communities and, increasingly, among Asians. There is self-interest. We thought having more women and more diversity would help us do better business."

In fact, he regrets not moving toward diversity earlier, given the changes in the marketplace in the last decade or so. "We have a high percentage of women in high places now. We had to work at it, to get women in the pipeline. If they had been there earlier, we might have seen sooner how those changes would affect us."

Avon deposits some of the returns of doing better business with its constituents. The company researched women's aspirations and the realities they face and discovered that the realities are often much grittier than the aspirations. The Avon Foundation, the philanthropic arm of the company, is now geared toward women's issues, especially women's health and education. The foundation sponsors a breast cancer prevention project that focuses on outreach and early detection.

Avon then is one of the most women-focused corporations in the country, interested in achieving balance not only for its workforce but with its consumer base. No doubt Preston would not be where he is today if he had not run into a woman who understood the glass ceiling and made its impact come alive. But having a muse like Patricia Neighbors at his shoulder persuaded Preston to take his company further than most.

process of developing those strategies, though, an organization almost necessarily looks into its heart and soul, uncovering strengths and areas of challenge. Even the startup process of evaluating the climate for women at an organization—digging out the data—will reveal objective information that may be put to other strategic uses as well. Ultimately, a gender initiative can give a company not just the best talent, but the best prospects as well.

2

Three of the Best

Most companies have several related reasons for deciding to advance women, but in virtually every company Catalyst works with, the immediate imperative is the change in expectations about and within the American workforce. From the employer's perspective, the talent available to companies and necessary to compete on a global stage will be more diverse, demographers project, than the traditional talent pool made up of white men. Business leaders are well aware that women, like other groups previously excluded from the business mainstream, offer a fresh viewpoint, a unique approach to business strategy, and a connection to emerging markets.

At the same time, employees—male and female—at all levels of work organizations are now much more willing than their traditional counterparts to seek a balance between their work and personal lives. Companies wanting the competitive advantage an expanded talent pool offers are taking steps to enhance their appeal as "employers of choice," the companies at which the most-talented people want to work.

Three such Catalyst Award–winning companies—Motorola, Deloitte & Touche, and the Bank of Montreal—represent a range of sizes, industries, and organizational types that all adopted a similar framework to encompass the best practices that would lead to change. Laying the groundwork for intentional change is critical.

17

Before embarking on a change initiative, a company should identify a clear problem to solve or goal to achieve; should be able to articulate the business rationale for undertaking change; have a commitment from the company's leadership to play an active, visible role; make extensive efforts to communicate the importance of the initiative, and decide who will be accountable for implementing and tracking the progress of the initiative. These steps create the conditions that make implementing best practices possible.

MOTOROLA, INC.

Electronics and wireless communication

Employees: 142,000

Annual revenues: $27 billion

Catalyst Award: 1993

Succession planning was well-entrenched at Motorola long before affirmative action or diversity became corporate issues. The Schaumberg, Illinois–based maker of electronic equipment, systems, and components always made sure to have "bench strength" in replacements down the chain of command, so that if key people left or were lost to illness, retirement, or death, another person would be ready to step in and keep the business going. Beginning in the late 1980s, however, motivated by changes in workplace demographics, Motorola redesigned its succession planning process to make leadership development of women and minorities a priority.

For many years, the succession planning process, known at Motorola as the Organization and Management Development Review (OMDR), had helped identify and develop high-potential managers for specific leadership roles. In 1991, OMDR was set the additional task of incorporating the company's diversity objectives; its mission was to accelerate the advancement of women and minorities in the organization. In adapting succession planning, company leaders set a ten-year deadline to bring the number of women and minorities in the company, at all levels of management, into parity with the available talent pool, especially on the first two rungs of succession. Although there was inadequate census information on the demographics of business executives, Motorola adopted "Officer Parity Goals," a commitment that every year at least three women and minorities would be among the twenty to forty people promoted to vice president.

Motorola's method of identifying high-potential managers guarantees that talented women and minorities as well as white men will enter and move along the succession pipeline. The company has developed a system to identify individuals who have the potential to be promoted two levels in five years—"high potentials" by Motorola's definition. Evaluation forms are sent out to each of Motorola's major operations and then distributed down through management.

Each division annually submits lists of up to twenty high-potential candidates, in four categories: white men, women, minorities, and technical staff. As the lists are passed back up the management ladder they are winnowed down. Managers must include career development plans for each high-potential individual. They are tracked by virtue of having been identified; if they leave the company or fall off the list, which is reevaluated every year, division leadership will ask the individual's manager to explain why.

The OMDR process also ensures that women and minorities are among those being groomed for senior positions in the company. An annual succession planning form, the replacement chart, identifies key positions and three people who could fill each one: line one is the immediate successor, the person who could step into the position immediately; line two is the person who should succeed the incumbent if the company had three to five years to prepare for the transition; line three is the most qualified woman or minority candidate at that time, in addition to any woman or minority person already on line one or two. Women and minorities must be included even if it means hiring from outside.

Making certain women and minorities are prominently on the replacement chart counters any perception that most women and minorities are still in the *feeder pool*, that is, too far back in the pipeline to be thought of for senior positions. "We had to get the 'feeder' people on the radar," says Roberta Gutman, a Motorola senior vice president who directs the corporate diversity initiative. "Once they were on the radar, we could ask very pointed development questions." Once on the company's radar, it is harder for people to disappear back down into feeder pools or dead-end career paths. "We put specific people on the radar so we could keep asking whatever happened to them," Gutman says.

Career Planning

Implicit in Motorola's succession planning structure is that individuals receive guidance that will help them set career goals and develop a plan to achieve them. Succession planning requires managers to help the employees they are responsible for plot a career course. The high-potential individual's career plan is likely to include such things as developmental rotations, which prepare her or him for senior leadership in the future. There has always been a great deal of informal mentoring, but now Motorola encourages its senior leadership to seek out opportunities to mentor women and minorities.

Women have had the benefit of the Women's Leadership Conference, a gathering organized around career issues relevant to women. The chief executive addresses the conference and several of Motorola's top female executives talk at workshops about topics like career growth, balance between personal and business life, women's leadership styles, mentoring and role models.

The Business Rationale

Motorola made the business case for the diversity initiative by establishing an explicit link between the company's pursuit of quality, productivity, new markets, and profits and the return an expanded, diverse talent pool would bring. Not only would the company have more talented people to choose from, it would also gain the perspective of groups that traditionally had not been in the managerial workforce in large numbers. At each level of organization, the initiative was linked to strategies, action plans, and results. In presentations to employees, senior management emphasized the connections among business success, creating or expanding new markets overseas, and having a socially diverse workforce.

Leadership's Role

Motorola believes senior management support for diversity programs is essential to its success. George M. C. Fisher, then Motorola's chief executive, and its president, Gary Tooker, who succeeded Fisher as chief executive, championed the initiative from the outset. Top management has gone through a gender awareness training program and several belong to the Premier Employer Council, the group responsible for addressing issues affecting employees, like work-family balance, diversity and carer development. Presidents of the major Motorola operations develop plans for meeting diversity goals within their units; the quarterly reports the managers in those divisions make on the status of women and minorities are passed on to the chief executive, who meets at least once a year with each division president specifically to discuss in detail the progress of the initiative.

Accountability

Motorola has embedded several accountability measures in the structure of the initiative. Among them importantly, the company believes that because diversity is a business initiative, line managers, not the human resources department, should be responsible for its implementation. Human resources does monitor and analyze the company's progress toward its parity goals, but senior managers are

Exhibit 2.1. Tying Diversity Goals to Action Plans

Mission (the reason we exist)	Objectives (the results we expect)	Strategies (how we do it)	1996 Action Plans (what we'll do)
Build . . . the organizational capability to tap the potential of all people needed to achieve business success.	Productivity . . . Increase the ability of current talent to contribute and influence business results.	Long-term, *large-scale* organizational change (culture, systems, behavior).	Build a *multicultural strategy* for globalization by year end.
	Resources . . . Increase the pool of available talent from which we can select.	*Expand* sponsorship to each leader-manager.	Assure *diverse leadership in place* to meet global business challenges.
	Creativity . . . A richer array of business options and ideas.	Design people systems to reflect the values, expectations, and experience of all our people.	Enhance *systems to limit company liability.*
Vision (the future we help create)	Market Opportunities . . . Mirror our customer base.	*Integrate* diversity into organizational effectiveness processes.	Explore how to integrate *principles of diversity* into organizational systems, processes, and behaviors.
	Communications . . . Increase the level of trust and respect.	*Develop* opportunities for all employees to influence this change.	Standardize and centralize *processes and presentations* to facilitate ease of transfer.
Capture the energy created by workforce diversity to achieve a unique global competence.	Compliance . . . Legally defensible systems in place to limit company liability.	*Set targets* for tracking, appraising, and rewarding managers.	Provide employees *opportunities* to gain awareness, develop skills, and influence the diversity change process.
	Balanced Workforce . . . Achieve parity in all management levels.	*Train* all employees on why and how to behave appropriately in a diverse workforce.	Define and include *behavioral objectives* in all individual career plans for three management tiers in three organizations.

responsible for developing and retaining the high-potential candidates under their supervision. Senior managers also are expected to keep track of and report on the representation of women and people of color in their units.

The seven business units within Motorola have the flexibility to decide what diversity goals are appropriate to the unit. Each unit president met regularly with Motorola's chief executive to report on the results of the initiative. Progress in diversity is one of several categories factored into the size of senior executive bonuses.

Results

In 1989, Motorola had two female vice presidents. In 1997, there were forty, including seven women of color.

The initiative has also had an impact on Motorola's corporate culture. The culture has always been supportive of individuals and seen their success as coextensive with the success of the company. But when the initiative began, Motorola was just beginning to shift to a participative management style from the more traditional hierarchical style. The diversity initiative has accelerated that change in style.

Key Elements

- Broad definition of succession planning to include the widest talent pool

- Careful and strategic planning for individual career development

- Strong leadership and commitment from senior management

- Clearly defined targets and goals

- Manager accountability for the initiative's success

- Integration of business and diversity objectives

DELOITTE & TOUCHE

Accounting and auditing, tax, and management consulting

Employees: 23,000

Annual revenues: $3.66 billion

Catalyst Award: 1995

Deloitte & Touche, the giant tax, auditing, and consulting firm, spends millions of dollars annually on recruiting and training. The cost of turnover is high, because when professionals D&T has brought along leave before fulfilling their potential, the firm loses the return on its investment in human capital. But turnover has a broader impact: it dampens productivity, interrupts client service, and may lower morale.

It was with these issues in mind that late in 1991, D&T's chief executive decided to find out why the firm seemed to have so few female candidates for partner and a disproportionately high turnover rate among its experienced, high-potential female professionals. Though men and women had entered accounting in equal numbers in the last decade and a half, after six to eight years only two women remained for every three men in the same hiring group. D&T's board of directors appointed the largely partner-level Task Force for the Retention and Advancement of Women to find out why women were leaving D&T at a faster rate than men. The task force, which began formally in January 1992, concentrated on three areas: the environment in which the firm operates, the perceived obstacles to success, and the necessity to balance the multiple commitments of professional and personal lives. In December 1992, the task force commissioned a work-life balance survey to assess the impact of balance issues on employees.

The survey revealed dissatisfaction among both women and men with their lives at work. The traditional markers of success seemed less enticing to the group surveyed than might have been expected;

even the notion of making partner was not universally extolled. Most of the group wanted more flexibility than the partnership track typically offered young professionals either to be with their children or simply to have more time for a personal life. At the same time, the business of consulting was changing rapidly. The firm was more likely to hire experienced people, who were also more likely to want flexibility in their work arrangements, usually to spend more time with their families.

In early 1993, its year of work done, the task force made several recommendations to the board of directors:

- Establish a leadership program

- Promote the idea of men and women as colleagues

- Enhance career opportunities for women

- Support the balance of multiple commitments

- Build goals and accountability into business planning and HR processes

- Communicate program activities and policy changes inside and outside the firm

These recommendations became the basis for D&T's Initiative for the Retention and Advancement of Women.

The Program

D&T's initiative has several interrelated pieces: communication, Men and Women as Colleagues workshops, the partner implementation network, support from the top, assignment review, flexible work arrangement policies, career development, and an external council of experts.

Communication: D&T has been unusually willing to communicate publicly about the initiative. J. Michael Cook, D&T's chief

J. Michael Cook, Chairman and CEO, Deloitte & Touche

Some chief executives talk the talk of diversity but not many of them walk the walk with as much determination as Mike Cook, head of Deloitte & Touche, the big tax, auditing, and consulting firm. Since the early 1990s, Cook has been one of the most visible advocates for gender diversity in business and the supporting programs that can make it a reality. The roots of his enthusiasm can be summarized in two words: *dropouts* and *daughters*.

When women started entering professional schools in large numbers in the 1970s and 1980s, Cook felt confident that it was only a matter of time before a critical mass of them would travel up along the pipeline and into the partner suite. By 1990, it was clear that was not happening. The firm was not seeing the results down the road of making half its entering classes female; the turnover rate for women was much higher than for men.

"You can't hire 50 percent of any group and have them leave in large numbers," Cook says. "We don't have products to sell, we have the talent of our people. We have to have high-talent people."

He assumed women were leaving to have families, but his daughters—both young women in business—set him straight. "They said, 'We are going to have careers,'" meaning they weren't planning to leave the workforce permanently or until the nest emptied. "It started to dawn on me that the pipeline wasn't going to push women along," he says. The pipeline was "leaking" women.

So instead of making assumptions based on a 1950s-in-aspic view of women, he got his people to go and ask the high-potential dropouts why they left. A combination of factors, they all said: the bruising culture of a big consulting firm, their perception that, as women, they would have few opportunities to advance—and the lack of flexibility in work arrangements.

What was needed, it became clear, was not just affirmative action but a corporate cultural shift. Led by Cook, D&T devised the Initiative for the Retention and Advancement of Women, which expanded the paths to success at the firm, loosened the thongs that had bound young professionals to their desks for twenty-four-hour days, and opened up the mysterious, all-important assigning processes wherein careers were made or lost.

The firm took the virtually unique step of transforming itself in public when it hired Lynn Martin, a diversity-consultant-cum-road-warrior since finishing her service as U.S. Secretary of Labor in the Bush administration, to head an external committee that would advise D&T.

The firm now is barely five years into the initiative, so Cook waves aside any question of when it will be finished. It has already seen a better balance in retention rates: turnover among younger professionals is roughly equal for men and women. Cook didn't and doesn't expect to get to 50 percent female partners in the first five to seven years of the initiative. "It's the pipeline that's not that robust," he says. But he believes D&T has fixed the leak that was letting women slip away and that the firm will see the fruits of the repair in the next few years, as the gender-equal classes arrive at the partner stage.

There will no longer be a need for an initiative, Cook says, when it intertwines with the firm's culture. He knows from his daughters that the expectations of the young are not what they were when he started out. He sees that at D&T as well. "These issues—being driven, working long hours—bother young people less than they did," he says. They want to know why allowing flexibility and differential career tracks flummoxes so many older professionals. "What's the big deal?" they want to know. Indeed, Cook's best hope is that when D&T has reached its initiative's goals, no one will notice—because they take an equitable and flexible work environment for granted.

executive, and Ellen Gabriel, national director for the advancement of women, have been interviewed extensively by the news media and have traveled around the country speaking about their approach. Internally, information on the initiative and its progress is communicated through newsletters, bulletins, and the annual report.

D&T says the high visibility of the initiative keeps the firm from backing away from its goals, so it is in part an accountability measure. The publicity has also elicited very positive responses from other big firms, and so acts as an antidote to backlash.

Men and Women as Colleagues: This is a program of gender awareness workshops held in offices across the country. Ninety-eight percent of managers, senior managers, and partners have participated.

Male and female professionals go through a two-day workshop designed to sensitize both groups to the perceptions they have or assumptions they make about each other. During the workshop, participants devise a list of areas that need to be worked on in their offices.

Many D&T employees view the workshops as the most compelling piece of the initiative. Participants consistently report they opened up a dialogue on issues that have made many people uncomfortable. Women now feel much more comfortable discussing their concerns, rather than staying silent and eventually leaving the company. Men and women seem to feel more comfortable discussing gender issues in general.

Assignment review: The task force found that one of the most significant obstacles to career advancement for women was the system by which assignments are made. Assignments determine skills, skills determine advancement. There was a perception that women were not assigned to the right positions on the right teams. Each office reviewed the assignments over the last few years, in an effort to make the process more equitable. This piece of the initiative was a creative way to get at the more subtle ways women were kept from access to the skills needed for advancement.

Flexible work arrangements: Using the work-life balance survey, a flexible work arrangements task force was able to develop a range of options, including flextime, reduced workload, and telecommuting. Ninety percent of the professionals who use the flexible work arrangement are female, but men increasingly are using the arrangement to take parental leave.

Career development: The initiative instituted written three-to-five-year career development plans for female senior managers and partners. Women and their supervisors put the plans together, and the plans are then reviewed by the group managing partners.

In addition, D&T has come to put greater emphasis on career planning for all professionals. The firm created a new position to run a leadership and management development program. It has also developed a new format for evaluating individuals about to make partner.

Leadership and Accountability

D&T's chief executive has played an active role in promoting the initiative's success, making numerous public appearances to articulate his firm's commitment to women. Acknowledging the importance of buy-in from the top down, D&T created the Partnership Implementation Network, made up of partners around the country, each chosen for his or her stature within the organization and commitment to the initiative. Each partner took responsibility for implementation of the initiative in at least one of the individual regional offices. In consultation with the partner, each office developed its own action plan.

In 1993, Ellen Gabriel (a senior executive) was named National Director for the Advancement of Women. She assumed leadership of the initiative. Two months later, the firm created the Council on the Advancement of Women and brought in Lynn Martin, the former Secretary of Labor, to be chairwoman. The council is composed of senior executives, leaders of the Women's Initiative Network, and a group of four outside experts who help keep D&T from veering from its objectives. It meets twice a year, and continues to advise the firm on the initiative. Ellen Gabriel emphasizes Martin's contribution to the plan's success: "She would tell people they had to change and make them want to do it."

To measure the initiative's progress, Deloitte & Touche has adopted several benchmark statistics, including a baseline head-count of the gender mix at the firm, the gender gap in turnover, pro-motion rates of women versus men, and the percentage of women coming in as experienced hires.

Results

Since the implementation of the initiative, the percentage of women admitted to partnership has increased from 8 percent in 1991 to 20 percent in 1997. Women partners now account for 10 percent of all partners, up from 5 percent in 1991. In addition, the gap in turnover rate between men and women has narrowed, par-ticularly at the higher levels (partner, senior manager, manager). Over seven hundred professionals take advantage of flexible work arrangements today, including fifteen partners. The firm has tripled the number of women in key leadership positions since 1993.

As its early proponents hoped, the initiative has had a signifi-cant impact on Deloitte & Touche's culture. Because of the Men and Women as Colleagues workshops, women feel more comfort-able raising issues related to advancement and partners feel an im-perative to discuss them. The organization shows a commitment to employees' career development. D&T reports that prior to the Women's Initiative, partners and those wanting to be partner would not have taken a reduced workload for fear of the stigma attached to that decision: a perceived lack of commitment or focus. As in-tended, says Ellen Gabriel, the initiative has affected all people at D&T positively.

Key Elements

- Forceful, visible leadership from the chief executive
- Senior-level accountability at all regional offices
- Clear relationship between the initiative's goals and the problem of turnover
- A well-thought-out strategy

BANK OF MONTREAL

Chartered bank

Employees: 34,826

Average assets: $147 billion

Catalyst Award: 1994

The Bank of Montreal, Canada's oldest chartered bank and one of the largest financial institutions in North America, undertook its gender initiative as part of a change in strategic direction that began in 1990. In a message to employees, the chairman, chief executive, and president of the bank underscored the importance of the relationship between highly talented employees and exceptional, cost-effective service and committed the bank to help staff develop their underutilized skills and talents by providing career guidance. The bank was particularly interested in cultivating women, who at that time made up 75 percent of its employee population but only 9 percent of its executive ranks.

The Business Rationale

The bank's business imperative was simple and clear: the increasing importance of customer service to the bank's success. Senior management saw that leadership in the traditional areas of competition—products and technology—could no longer guarantee industry leadership. In 1989, when the bank's new leadership began plotting out a long-term corporate strategy, it decided to make the Bank of Montreal, in the words of one article, "the bank of choice for employees." That meant attracting, keeping, and promoting the best employees it could find.

Leadership's Role

Early in 1991, F. Anthony Comper, the bank's president and chief operating officer, commissioned the Employee Task Force on the Advancement of Women to identify barriers to female advancement and to devise strategies to break them down. The mandate of the task force was to "identify the constraints to the advancement of women" and to "recommend goals and measures." It added, "Don't just give us theory; give us action plans so we can really effect change."

The bank's investigative phase broke new ground as part of a women's initiative. The task force reviewed the human resource data base, interviewed 270 people, performed eleven focus groups, and surveyed five hundred former managers. But the most important thing it did was a survey of fifteen thousand women and men employees, asking such questions as "What is the #1 thing that's holding women back?" and "What would you like the bank to do to help you advance?" The key finding from the task force: "Women were not advancing because of stereotypical attitudes, myths of conventional wisdom."

The task force set out on a "myth-busting" venture, countering each of the myths with facts gleaned from the human resources files. For example, "We would love to promote women if they had the proper education" was countered with the fact that the women in the bank were as educated as the men. Another myth—"Women have babies and quit; they're not committed to their careers"—was countered with the statistic that 98 percent of women who have children return to the bank. The most common erroneous assumptions about women's failure to advance in the bank's executive ranks, as revealed by the survey, were

- Women at the bank are either too young or too old to compete equitably with men.

- Because of child-rearing responsibilities, women are less committed to their careers.

- Women do not have the educational credentials to compete with men.

- Women don't have "the right stuff" to compete for senior jobs.

- Women haven't been in the pipeline long enough to advance to senior levels.

- Time will take care of the problem.

What the task force learned was that all the myths and stereotypes were patently false and required refutation. As a result of its myth-busting, the bank was able to demonstrate that women are equally as qualified, equally as educated, and equally as committed as men. The survey also found that women and men were similar in the initiatives they would like to enable them to advance. Both talked about needing flexibility in scheduling work hours, both wanted to have control of careers and wanted information about management vacancies, and both sought mentoring.

Communication

To lay the groundwork for eliminating barriers to women's advancement, the task force issued a report with information about female employees at the bank. Based on the survey research and the analysis of demographic data on male and female employees, the report used a myths-and-realities approach and was distributed to all staff. It included this information:

- On average, women and men are the same age.

- Although women have babies and more responsibility for childrearing, they have longer service records at the bank, except at senior levels.

- An analysis of performance appraisals revealed that a higher percentage of women than men were ranked in the top two tiers of each level.

- The percentage of women in senior positions has grown so slowly—1 percent a year—that it is not practical to wait for time to take care of the problem.

Program

The bank's initiative to recruit, retain, and advance women combines concern for gender diversity and for making work arrangements more flexible. The initial task force recommended that the bank establish a senior-level position, a Vice President for Workplace Equality, that would be responsible for the initiative, as well as a Workplace Equality Team that could provide advice and information from headquarters and the eight regional units of the bank. The bank did both; it also set up a tracking system for evaluating the initiative and agreed to institutionalize employee feedback. Because the original survey indicated many employee perceptions were at odds with reality, the bank has been vigilant in communicating the impact of the initiative. "We try to be sensitive to new myths that get created," said Elizabeth Spencer, a manager of workplace equality at the bank. "When we heard that some men felt they were no longer receiving promotions, we published the reality, which is that men as well as women get promoted."

The initiative itself has several components, roughly arrayed into training, career planning and performance review, and flexible work arrangements.

Training: The bank has incorporated "Managing Diversity" and "Men and Women as Colleagues" into its management training curriculum and added a leadership curriculum to help managers develop a leadership style that emphasizes coaching and teamwork. It has also instituted several specialized accreditation programs to help men and women gain credentials that will help them advance. The program addresses historical inequities in employment, in which women were concentrated in personal banking, with limited authority on how much they could lend. The bank's goal is for half the trainees in each program to be female.

Bank of Montreal has also developed computer-assisted self-learning courses for branch staff to increase their knowledge and skill base and become eligible for more senior positions.

The bank has set up a career information network that provides listings of job vacancies for mid-to-senior management positions. There is also a job posting system for regional positions in lower-level jobs.

Flexible work arrangements: Employees are able to work out flexible arrangements with their supervisors. "Flexing Your Options," a manual distributed to all employees, including managers, offers detailed advice on how to implement a flexible work arrangement.

Results

In six years, from late 1991 to late 1997, the representation of women in executive ranks increased from 9 percent to 24 percent. Among senior vice presidents, women have increased from 3 percent to 27 percent, and their representation among senior management has increased from 13 percent to 26 percent.

The bank has just introduced a recognition initiative, sponsored by the president and the President's Council (a group of senior executives), where employees have been invited to nominate colleagues who deserve recognition as champions for their efforts on behalf of diversity.

Key Elements

- Regular assessment of employee attitudes and perceptions

- Immediate research and quick dissemination of facts to dispel misperceptions

- Broad and strategic communications program, internal and external

- Support from the bank's chief executive and other senior leaders

Joseph A. Pichler, Chairman and CEO, the Kroger Company

Many may believe it, but not many chief executives feel it is wise to admit they support diversity because it is the right and proper thing to do. For Joseph Pichler, chief executive of Kroger—the nation's largest supermarket chain—diversity is, as he calls it, "a religious and moral moment." The religious training he received at a Jesuit high school and later at Notre Dame provided him with a strong moral argument for equality of opportunity.

The doctorate in labor economics he received later from the University of Chicago gave him the bottom-line argument for diversity more commonly heard among chief executives. "I did a lot of work on discrimination. The market-efficiency as well as the moral arguments for opening up opportunities became very clear," he says.

He took this perspective with him to Kroger, which operates supermarkets and convenience stores in the Midwest and Sun Belt, and gathered a team around him to revamp the structure of opportunity at the chain. The supermarket industry in other parts of the country has been cited for its reluctance to modify several decades of practices that virtually excluded women from management. Pichler said he found a lot of good will at Kroger.

To make the change, several programs were started, but perhaps the most important action the company took early on was to identify the lynchpin job for promotion: the store manager. Women were not getting store manager jobs, which were the ones that would put them in the pipeline, so Kroger instituted an accountability system: quarterly reviews of all candidates for store manager by race and gender. If the stores have no female or minority candidates, they have to explain why.

Kroger accepted in principle—Pichler never minds returning to principle—that its number-one nonfinancial goal would be to increase opportunities in operating management positions for women and minorities. The opening up of opportunity has to become an instinctual movement if an initiative is to succeed, Pichler contends.

When Pichler offers advice to other companies looking to establish diversity initiatives, he still puts the moral argument first, though he will stipulate that business and legal reasons may also be persuasive. His "lean" theory of management—perhaps based on the Jesuits' view that reasoned argument and muscular persistence will always carry the day—leads him to say, "The important thing is not how people feel, but how they behave. You want them to behave right. You can't crawl into anyone's head. You set out the path, monitor it, and keep leaning on it," he says. "They'll come around."

3

Benchmarking:
Tool to Foster Women's Advancement

In American business organizations, what is valued gets measured, or as some companies put it, "we measure what we treasure." Historically, companies' measurement systems focused on their profit centers—products, production processes, and customer satisfaction, while employees were regarded as expenses. More recently, management initiatives have required companies to invest in training and in empowering employees to participate in decision making at all levels of the organization, thus transforming the view of employees from cost to profit centers.

Leveraging their investment in employee recruitment and development is a growing concern of companies and professional firms. This has led to increased interest and activity around measuring the effectiveness of human resources management. Today, companies are concerned about measuring how they are doing in attracting, retaining, developing, and advancing to leadership roles the best and brightest talent available. Indeed, in 1997, measuring human resources management outcomes is the leading form of benchmarking activity engaged in by American business organizations. Within the broad arena of human resources management, benchmarking diversity practices and outcomes not only has gained interest, but also has become integral to some of America's leading companies and firms.

Benchmarking, when instituted comprehensively, is a three-step program that begins with an organization's learning about its own practices and outcomes, learning about the best practices of others, and making change for improvement that will enable it to compete with the best in the world. Just knowing how another company does something is not enough; benchmarking is not an end in itself. It is intended to make change and to arm organizations with the information needed to make that change. Most organizations find that benchmarking works best when it is part of a process of continuous improvement and a comprehensive strategy.

Gender Diversity Benchmarking

The goals of benchmarking women's advancement are twofold: to improve a company's competitive advantage in recruiting, retaining, and developing diverse talent so as to enhance business results, and to provide a corporate culture and work environment where everyone has equal access to opportunities and equal encouragement to contribute and succeed. This means looking at the key performance areas of recruitment, retention, development, and advancement outcomes, as well as at qualitative outcomes such as employee job satisfaction, optimism about future opportunities for advancement, and other measures of morale and commitment to the employing organization.

Specific objectives of benchmarking women's advancement include

- Creating the business case for gender diversity
- Tying diversity strategies to short- and long-term business imperatives and strategic business plans
- Identifying and recruiting the best and brightest talent
- Eliminating barriers to success
- Enhancing access to opportunities

Phase I: Internal Benchmarking

Benchmarking women's advancement involves two major areas of research activity: internal and external research benchmarking. Most discussions of benchmarking focus on external benchmarking. This is the process of gathering information on the gender diversity practices and outcomes of industry peers, competitors, or companies with the recognized best practices. Internal benchmarking—the process of gathering information on practices and outcomes within one's own organization—typically receives less attention in the literature on benchmarking. Yet Catalyst finds that internal benchmarking is equally important—if not more important—than external benchmarking in preparing a company or firm for the transformation process that follows benchmarking research.

Partners in various functional areas within the organization carry out internal benchmarking—sometimes referred to as functional benchmarking—by using existing data or new data generated by benchmarking research. This involves looking at what the organization is actually doing to identify both ineffective practices and best practices for advancing women. Companies and firms sometimes express surprise at learning that best practices exist within their own operating units—practices that, if rolled out to other business units, would make significant positive changes in the organization's overall environment for women. Internal benchmarking also uncovers areas of inconsistency in gender diversity performance outcomes across functional areas or business units.

Internal research provides meaningful metrics that enable companies to do the following:

- Establish the current status of women at the organization, reviewing such information as recruitment, retention and advancement.

- Develop short- and long-term goals for improvement after the process of external benchmarking is concluded.

- Evaluate the effectiveness of initiatives that result from benchmarking by measuring and reporting progress toward specified goals.

Thus before it even begins to look at external data, the organization gains a concrete sense of *where* and *what* it is doing well and not so well in gender diversity. Without this information, it is impossible to carry out successful external benchmarking.

Internal Benchmarking—Quantitative Measures

While it is fairly easy to develop quantitative measures for a variety of gender diversity areas, many companies either do not maintain such data or have not designed their human resources management information systems in a way that enables them to look at different components of women's advancement in relation to each other. For example, compensation, benefits, leave, and promotion data may be separately maintained and reported. It is also fairly common for companies to have a general sense of the representation of women and people of color by levels within the organization, but not to know how they are represented across functions or business areas, and not to know where there is disproportionate attrition of employees in these groups.

Research by Catalyst and others shows that cross-functional development opportunities are one of the requisites for advancement in corporations and firms; the lack thereof prevents women and people of color from competing for the highest-level positions in their organization. However, many companies do not know the extent to which women are represented in line or staff positions. Research also shows that while entry-level male and female managers and professionals generally receive comparable compensation packages, a wage gap between men and women frequently develops as they advance within the organization, one that cannot always be explained by differences in tenure or performance. Compensation studies can uncover differences in the way women are rewarded for their contributions.

Another important performance area that should be examined in assessing gender diversity performance is the whole complex of activities around performance appraisal, career pathing, and access to opportunities. A simple measure of the effectiveness of career development systems is a comparison of the representation of gender diversity in the top three tiers of management versus the management pipeline as a whole. Internal benchmarking activities in this area, such as those at the Bank of Montreal, establish that time alone will not remedy women's lack of representation in senior management. As demonstrated by *Women in Corporate Leadership: Progress and Prospects*, it is more subtle environmental factors like stereotyping and exclusion from informal networks that impede women's progress; internal benchmarking uncovers these factors.

Organizations should also examine their succession planning processes to determine whether men or women are making it onto slates of candidates, and more important, whether their names reappear on slates year after year without explanation for their lack of mobility. Time in grade is another quantitative measure of managers' effectiveness in developing diverse talent. In the words of a Fortune 500 CEO: "In the case of women, we use the lack of specific training for a job as a reason not to open the jobs to them, when we are more ready to bring men into jobs for which they are not specifically trained. That kind of discrimination or stereotyping is much subtler and more difficult to get at."

Another important area for which an organization may develop quantitative measures is utilization of programs designed to help employees balance work and dependent care responsibilities, such as leaves and flexible work arrangements. Although companies may have excellent policies and programs in these areas, different functional areas and business units across the company may not implement them consistently. Catalyst's *Knowing the Territory: Women in Sales*, for example, shows that corporate leave and flexibility programs are underutilized in field offices due to manager resistance and lack of corporate oversight. This results in disproportionate turnover of women sales representatives.

George M. C. Fisher, Chairman, President, and CEO, Eastman Kodak Company

No company, not even a perennial favorite, can rest on its reputation and past success. It must find new worlds to conquer. In the case of Eastman Kodak, that is literally true. "A lot of our growth is outside the United States," says George Fisher, Eastman Kodak's chief executive. "We need a diverse workforce."

Diversity, he says, has become a global issue, an issue of different cultures as well as the more familiar categories of race and gender. For Kodak until recently, "diverse" has meant accelerating the progress of women and members of minority groups and providing support systems to make flexible work arrangements possible. Fisher notes that Kodak has a "big consumer presence and many female customers. A large fraction of our commercial customers are women," he says. So whether the market is predominantly female or international, the principle is the same: "From a marketing standpoint, it makes sense to have someone who looks at the world through the lens of the group you're trying to sell to, who is likely to have a connection," he says.

Although Fisher speaks with urgency about diversity, it is not the urgency of the newly converted. He encountered diversity training early in his career, at Bell Labs. When he was chief executive at Motorola, Fisher championed a diversity initiative that opened up the technology company's succession-planning process. Maintaining an outstanding talent pool, Motorola figured out how to increase the representation of women and minorities at all the stops along the pipeline to the executive suite.

As a long-term champion and observer of diversity, Fisher has seen attitudes toward the issue change. There is much more acceptance now, even though there is still a wide spectrum of response. "There is almost no negative response now, but the degree of acceptance ranges from passive to proactive," he says. The problem is less bringing people on board to accept the rationality of diversity as a business strategy than it is achieving gains once a program is in place. "It's not hard to lead, it's hard to achieve significant gains. In times when companies are restructuring and having layoffs or selling off parts of the business, it is hard to keep going in the direction you want to go," he says. "In tough times it can fall off the chart."

Fisher is determined not to let the issue fall off the chart, even as Kodak ventures out into relatively uncharted international waters. Kodak's focus has been to increase the numbers of women and minorities in management ranks until they reflect an appropriate percentage of the company's potential talent pool. The company is paying particular attention to overseas assignments, which have taken on increasing importance. The goal is to expand the new perspective to include the entire Kodak workforce, to move out of the suites and into the factories. Kodak may well become the first vertically integrated internationally diverse company.

These measures, in combination, move a company in the direction of understanding how women are positioned in the organization and whether they are likely to be able to compete for top-level jobs without deliberate intervention to improve the opportunity structure of the organization.

Internal Benchmarking—Qualitative Measures

Internal benchmarking also involves understanding how different employee groups perceive the corporate culture and work environment. Organizations sometimes neglect this aspect of gender diversity performance when they perform internal benchmarking. In their efforts to develop a data-based business approach, they fail to understand the importance of employee perceptions regarding diversity performance in the corporate culture and work environment. Yet we know that, for most people, perceptions are reality.

Qualitative research involves collecting data about employees' subjective experience and evaluations of the corporate culture and work environment. This *feeling* side of the work experience affects employees' decisions about joining and staying with an organization, as well as their career commitment, organizational loyalty, morale, and a host of other variables that ultimately have an impact on productivity and profitability. Thus they are important to measure. Together with other data—such as statistics on diversity representation and retention, program utilization, compensation studies, and so on—research on employees' experience, perceptions, and opinions enables companies to make better decisions and thus improve diversity performance.

Qualitative gender diversity performance measures focus on employee satisfaction in the following areas:

- Work environment in general

- Content of specific jobs

- Access to developmental opportunities

- Support from supervisors
- Constructive feedback on performance
- Access to mentors
- Recognition and reward systems
- Optimism about future opportunities for career growth and advancement

Affiliation, participation, and perceptions of empowerment are also factors that have an impact on performance outcomes for women's advancement.

Many of the opportunities associated with advancement to senior ranks in companies are accessed through informal networks and channels of communication. Historically, women have lacked access to the informal opportunity structure, as confirmed by Catalyst's survey of senior management women, *Women in Corporate Leadership*, where women listed the most critical obstacles to their advancement as male stereotyping and preconceptions and female exclusion from informal networks. To assess various employee groups' perceptions of access to informal opportunities, companies and firms use surveys, focus groups, and individual interviews. An analysis of performance appraisal forms can identify disparities in the feedback, evaluation, and career coaching that supervisors provide to men and women in the organization. In addition, content analysis of corporate communications can establish whether women are getting exposure for their contributions. In this vein, an analysis of how the organization announces promotions can provide insight into the shaping of male perceptions—and attendant backlash—about the advancement of women.

There are several other research activities that can prove useful:

- *Cohort analysis.* This provides an examination of the career paths of "classes" of men and women recruited to entry-level positions in the organization at year three, year five, and year ten, or at other specified career checkpoints. How have women progressed relative to men with similar backgrounds and credentials? To what extent have men and women had equal opportunities to work on both line and staff sides of the organization? Who is most likely to have been given critical assignments on task forces or in high-visibility work groups? It there a higher rate of attrition for women?

- *Officer career path assessment.* This diagrams the career paths of individuals who have reached the highest levels of leadership in the organization to determine what credentials are valued, what critical assignments position managers for advancement, and whether there are seats that most managers occupy en route to the top. This type of research enables companies to confirm or dispel beliefs about historic leadership profiles (for example, all top management come out of engineering, sales, or another area) and to begin to identify competencies that will be critical to future corporate leadership needs. This, in turn, will affect career development strategies and leadership profiles. Too frequently, the "do as I did" model of career development operates to exclude women from consideration for developmental assignments and promotions.

Catalyst has developed two metrics against which companies can measure their success nationwide in advancing women in corporate management and governance: annual censuses of women corporate officers and board directors of Fortune 500 companies. These metrics provide not only a national measurement and progress report on women at individual companies, by industry, and for the group of companies as a whole; they also provide individual companies with data with which to compare themselves to industry peers and leading companies in other industries.

At the conclusion of an internal benchmarking process, a company or firm should be able to answer these two questions:

- What and where are we doing well in gender diversity performance areas critical to our business?

- Where do we need improvement?

Equally important, internal benchmarking also provides critical data from which the organization can shape its specific business case for improving gender diversity performance. As discussed in Chapter Two, internal benchmarking at Deloitte & Touche documented the high level and cost of turnover of female professionals in the firm and became a central component of the business case for change articulated by CEO J. Michael Cook.

The scope of the research undertaken during internal benchmarking will vary according to what measurements and monitoring data were available at the project's start versus what data need to be collected. The research's scope also will depend on the short- and long-term goals established by the project team responsible for benchmarking. There is no one right way of internal benchmarking, just as there is no one perfect external practice that can be adopted by every company. Each company must find its own way through the process guided by both employee and business needs and other contextual factors.

When an organization reaches this point, it has completed two basic action steps:

- Identification and communication of the business case for gender diversity.

- Identification of performance areas needing improvement.

It is now time to consider external benchmarking.

Phase II: External Benchmarking

External benchmarking is costly in terms of both financial and people resources, requiring a considerable degree of commitment by the organization. The action steps involved in external benchmarking include

1. Identification of companies to benchmark against.

2. Collection, analysis, and evaluation of data from these companies.

3. Determining the fit between best practices of other companies and contextual factors in the company doing the benchmarking: values, culture, business strategy, market position, morale, financial and human resources capabilities, technology, and so on.

4. Tailoring selected initiatives to the company's specific business needs.

5. Implementing initiatives.

6. Assigning accountability for monitoring and results.

7. Fine-tuning initiatives.

8. Continuing evaluation and measurement of gender diversity performance outcomes and identification of changing business needs.

The benchmarking task force. The external benchmarking team should be a manageable size—from five to eight members—with the understanding that it may call on additional expertise when needed without increasing the size of the core team. When designing selection criteria for the benchmarking committee or task force, the organization should consider two questions:

• Do we have the required expertise on the team to analyze and evaluate the data in the performance areas being addressed?

• Do we have the required clout on the team to authorize the deployment of organizational resources and to drive the recommendations through the organization at the conclusion of the research process?

Companies for benchmarking. Interviewing and visiting representatives of companies against which an organization is benchmarking is costly to both the company doing the research and the other organizations. Many world-class companies are weary of requests for benchmarking. The goal should be to identify only a few external benchmarking partners and to make the best choices. As Jac Fitz-Enz, an expert on benchmarking practices, observed in the April 1997 *H.R. Focus,* "Copy-catting someone else's best practice is not best practice. . . . Most best practices are not visible processes. . . . What you see on benchmarking tours usually are not essential elements. . . . You need to find the 'heart' of an initiative." The challenge for benchmarking teams is to identify the contextual factors that contribute to the initiative's effectiveness and to discern whether the initiative could be tailored to their own organization.

Phase III: Making Change

Catalyst's experience in benchmarking gender diversity practices in a wide range of business and professional organizations shows conclusively that isolated programs transplanted to new environments usually don't work. For example, there is limited value in implementing generous dependent care leave policies without flexibility of work scheduling and work sites; training is useful as part of a comprehensive career development system, but produces only limited, short-term change as a stand-alone approach. No turnkey gender diversity initiatives exist, although it is true that isolated programs can be copied or purchased "off the shelf." An organization should not be tempted to leap to easy solutions, diversity structures, or training before gender diversity is secured as part of the business plan and the real issues have been identified.

Pilots. Once organizations have selected and tailored appropriate practices, many choose to pilot the initiative in one or a small number of operational areas or geographic locations prior to performing a full-scale roll-out. This allows the benchmarking team to evaluate the impact of the initiative in its own corporate culture

Figure 3.1. Integrated Initiative Targets Culture Change

Maximize Workforce Value

Fundamental Culture Change

Accountability	Top Management Commitment	Measurement
Supporting Programs:		Supporting Education:
• Women's leadership development • Work-life supports • Core programs, policies, and values	Communicate the Vision	• Gender dynamics workshops • Feedback and coaching training
Economic Imperative		Clear Goals and Metrics

Conceptual Framework

and to fine-tune aspects of the initiative before widespread implementation. Some companies look for best- or worst-case environments in which to pilot the initiative in order to identify positive sources of support or opposition and to provide a comparative framework to measure outcomes.

Accountabilities and commitment from the top. Assigning accountability is key to the success or failure of any new initiative introduced into organizations, but this is especially critical for diversity initiatives. Accountability for implementation and positive outcomes must be articulated by the CEO and other senior line leadership in the organization. But everyone must realize that gender diversity initiatives require a long-term commitment, willingness to innovate and take risks, openness to partnering, the will to stay the course, and authority to release financial and people resources. All of these are roles that belong to senior leadership.

Typically, human resources professionals cochampion initiatives but have different accountabilities. HR works with senior line managers and the CEO to articulate the business case; it provides training, coaching, and other forms of "soft technology" to middle managers who are responsible for implementing initiatives; and it monitors both numerical and qualitative results.

To implement accountability systems, the task force or committee needs to clarify the roles of the CEO, chairman, senior line managers, other managers, human resources professionals, diversity networks, individual employees, and outside consultants in ensuring the success of the initiatives. It is not unusual for the CEO to establish a direct reporting relationship to one human resources professional who monitors and reports back on the implementation process, on the initial impact of initiative, and on its ongoing performance outcomes. (See the writeups on Bank of Montreal and Deloitte & Touche in the Benchmarking Culture section of Part II.)

Communication. As is critical with all organizational processes, the women's initiative needs to have a built-in communication plan. Some companies assign accountability for an initiative's communication strategy to one senior individual in the organization (as described in the writeup on Allstate in the Benchmarking Culture section of Part II). Specific communication needs include

- Communicating the findings from internal and external benchmarking

- Articulating the company's commitment to women at early stages of implementation when results may not be evident

- Producing a blueprint of the initiative and the business imperative behind it (as described in the writeup of Dow Chemical in the Work-Life Practices section of Part II)

- Outlining near- and long-term goals and action steps

Jerry Choate, CEO, Allstate Insurance Companies

Jerry Choate, chief executive of Allstate, can make all the arguments for hiring a diverse workforce. "The marketplace is getting more and more diverse. If we have diverse employees at every step of the organization, we can take advantage of it," he says.

But Choate can just as easily turn the argument around and explain why diversity motivates employees—especially when a workforce is, like Allstate's, 52 percent female. "Women have to have a sense that there is a future here for them. The same is true of minorities. They need role models, and to feel that it doesn't matter what their ethnicity or gender is—they can get ahead here," he says.

Some may find this surprising talk from the leader of a once-conservative company in one of the most buttoned-down of all industries. Allstate, though, seems to be taking a zippier

---

- Providing information on the availability and prerequisites for participating in specific programs related to the initiative, such as part-time work arrangements, telecommuting, dependent care leaves, and training

- Measuring and reporting progress toward goals as described in the writeup on Texas Instruments in the Women's Advancement section of Part II

Catalyst's extensive experience suggests the following lessons for companies undertaking a benchmarking initiative:

- There are no quick fixes.

- There is limited value in implementing isolated programs.

approach to business since it was spun off from its parent Sears Roebuck & Company in 1993. And certainly even a buttoned-down industry needs to attract the best employees.

Choate acknowledges that changes in family structure and demographics have come to the heartland. Allstate, he says, is just facing reality to get the best people. "Balancing work and life is getting more complicated. We have to help our employees do that. The old family model is over. We have to respond to that," he says. Allstate has responded with one of the most thorough diversity initiatives of any company in the country. It includes a child care center and flextime to help Allstate's many single-parent and dual-career families juggle their obligations.

The issue for the company is one of attracting talent. "When you're pretty much at full employment, you have to maximize your talent," Choate says. Allstate is doing that by giving everyone the opportunity to succeed.

- It is imperative that companies articulate the connection between business and diversity goals.

- Compliance is insufficient as a business case.

- There is real value in partnerships, such as the American Business Collaboration for Quality Dependent Care.

- Ad hoc best practices exist within every company that could be replicated on a systematic basis. To do so would improve diversity performance outcomes.

Above all, initiatives need to focus in the near term on changing behaviors, while working consistently toward long-term cultural and attitudinal change.

Paul A. Allaire, Chairman and CEO, Xerox Corporation

Some might say Paul Allaire was lucky to have worked overseas for Xerox from 1970 to 1983. After all, he missed shag haircuts, the beanbag chair, disco, and Billy Carter. But Allaire, who is now the chief executive of Xerox, missed a few other, equally momentous trends. When he returned to the United States, strange beings wandered the corporate landscape, whose like had rarely been seen before. "When I left, we didn't have women sales representatives. By 1983, we did," he says. "The world looked quite different when I came back."

Since the 1960s, Xerox had had a commitment to making members of minority groups, particularly black men, feel comfortable at the company. It did not start focusing on women until the 1980s. By the time he took over the company's leadership, it was clear to Allaire the company would have to make the same sort of explicit commitment to women. "With minorities, we have a balance; it's fairly consistent down the line," he says. "With women, we're not as good as we need to be."

Benchmarking is never really over. Internal benchmarking provides a snapshot of what and how well your company or firm is doing in terms of women's advancement. External benchmarking provides a snapshot of what and how well other companies are doing in the areas your benchmarking addresses. But diversity performance is a moving picture. Each year, the composition of employee populations shifts in subtle ways. Each year, new areas of difference enter—or emerge within—an organization. And each year that we work at improving diversity performance, the bar gets raised. This has been our experience with benchmarking at Catalyst.

Continuous improvement is a relentless process. Measuring and monitoring must be ongoing and will require fine-tuning existing

But, Allaire says, the earlier commitment provides a platform to build on. "It was the same thought process. The best minds don't come in a white male descriptor. They come in all races and genders," he says. The Xerox sales force is about equally balanced, but higher up, at the officer level, women have about 18 percent representation.

The critical commitment is to get in for the long term. "You can pluck a few people and drop them in, but in the long term, you have to have a base," Allaire says. And if the environment isn't friendly to women, the base isn't sustainable.

As he learned by moving abroad years ago, the world is constantly changing. It gets harder and harder to find men who haven't had women bosses—a once-unthinkable arrangement. And younger people have less patience for the sanctity of corporate tradition and learning the rules of the game. Young women are the leading edge of that change, Allaire believes. Face time, for example, has taken a real beating. "Young women say that's really dumb," Allaire says. "'I've got a family. I'll do the work I need to do, but I'm not going to hang around just to be seen.' They are refreshingly honest."

approaches and development of new initiatives. Openness to innovation, risk, and even failure in pursuit of excellence are givens for the companies that want to be the best. But while the demands are great, so are the rewards. In the words of one CEO whose company is committed to gender diversity, "The winners are going to be the organizations that view diversity as truly a mechanism to gain competitive advantage. If you have a richer senior management decision-making process, where more views are expressed easily and incorporated easily into decision making, you are going to wind up with better decisions."

Part II

Best Practices

This portion of the book is dedicated to descriptions of best practices that Catalyst has selected, based on benchmarking activities carried out through our basic research activities, proprietary research, and advisory services in individual companies and firms, as well as extensive involvement with corporate change initiatives nominated for the Catalyst Award. These best practices have been demonstrated to improve women's advancement at the organizations where they are used, and they have produced measurable results. They provide examples of approaches that have been used in a wide array of industries and professional services firms.

Initiatives, programs, and processes—rather than companies—are profiled because they can be replicated, with appropriate modifications, in companies seeking to improve their diversity performance. The Catalyst Award focuses on gender initiatives rather than "the best companies for women" because we know there are no perfect companies. Companies approach women's advancement and development in a variety of ways; no one way would be right for every company. Each practice could potentially stand on its own, and it may make sense for a company to begin with one program it can use as a platform to build on. A corporate culture cannot be replicated, whereas these component parts of existing initiatives for advancing women can be. We present these best practices with thanks to the companies whose generative leadership brought them into being and whose commitment sustains them.

Companies can benchmark against other organizations without singling out particular best practices. Some companies, for example, want only to identify the parameters of performance in a specific area of activity (such as compensation or benefits) so as to locate themselves somewhere in the middle of the pack. In effect, they make a deliberate decision not to be the best in that area.

Companies interested in benchmarking diversity best practices, as with other best practice benchmarking, are deliberately choosing to understand how the undisputed leaders in the area of women's advancement do it. They want to lead the pack or compete for leadership with the best. The practices for women's advancement included here are, we believe, genuine best practices, based on our extensive benchmarking within and across industries.

Some of the best practices described here may seem obvious or appear to be simple to implement—until one examines the context in which they have been developed and operationalized. Some industries have been difficult if not hostile business environments for women to enter and advance: mail-package-freight delivery, securities, computer software, food services, airlines, engineering, construction, computer data services, trucking, and pipelines. The annual *Catalyst Census of Women Board Directors of the Fortune 500* reports that certain industry areas continue to show the lowest representation of women at the board table, as well. Companies in these industries are starting at a different level of performance; it follows that their best practices may appear rudimentary, that is, focused on programmatic approaches to issues like recruitment or child care as opposed to more comprehensive initiatives.

The best practices profiled in this volume offer something for companies who are just starting out benchmarking women's advancement and those who have been working at improving their outcomes for a number of years. The book includes approaches from a number of industries, including those where the representation of women is fairly significant such as professional firms and services companies, and those where recruitment and advancement of women continues to be a challenge.

Even as this is being written, companies are trying new approaches. Catalyst has presented the most effective practices it is currently aware of. Companies should benchmark themselves against other best-practice companies and leverage their experience.

Most companies that have implemented leadership development programs for women use at least one, and often more than one, of the following:

- Flexibility in arranging work schedules and sites (flexible work arrangements)

- Removal of cultural and environmental barriers to women's advancement

- Early identification of high-potential women

- Leadership development for women that emphasizes lateral moves and line experience

Benchmarking Culture

The mission, beliefs, value systems, policies, rituals, tools, and philosophies of a corporation make up its culture. Though a company may have distinctive subcultures with differing values and beliefs, the corporate culture comprises the principles of the organization that are shared by most employees. The corporate culture is one aspect of the corporate environment, which includes all the physical conditions, circumstances, and influences surrounding and affecting individuals in a corporation or firm, including factors external to the organization that have an impact on its functioning.

Women's Advancement

Leadership development is the process by which individuals are provided with the training and experiences needed to assume increasing levels of responsibility within their company. Key leadership development experiences include profit and loss responsibility, learning to direct and motivate subordinates, gaining lateral cooperation, learning how the business works, standing alone, building and using structure and control systems, learning to be tough, persevering under adverse conditions, learning strategies and negotiation tactics, finding alternatives in solving and framing problems, and managing former peers or supervisors.

Upward mobility in corporations involves being selected for and performing successfully in a series of positions that involve increasing responsibility and accountability for business results. There is considerable variation in the way companies approach leadership development and upward mobility for women. Some companies believe that ensuring that women have equal access to training and other corporate development programs will suffice. Other companies have designed programs specifically for women, and still other companies have designed programs that address specific needs of women (and often minorities as well) but make them available to all employees whose performance and tenure qualify them for participation.

Many of the initiatives include explicit provision for formal mentoring arrangements. The word *mentor* is generally understood to mean a trusted counselor or guide. With mentoring's application to business, however, its definition and significance have grown more complicated. The classic mentor-protégé relationship in business is hierarchical in both age and experience. Generally, the responsibility of a mentor is to provide the protégé with the recognition, attention, and guidance she needs for optimum personal and professional growth.

A mentor may serve as a sponsor who nominates and helps advance the candidacy of a protégé for a promotion, pulling the protégé up through the organization. A mentor may also act as a coach, instructing the protégé on the training she needs to accomplish her career objectives and the skills her competition possesses. At times, the mentor may perform the role of protector, intervening or providing guidance to help the protégé avoid difficult situations.

Work-Life Practices

Among the work-family initiatives that have been implemented in companies and professional firms are parental and other dependent care–related leaves, sick leave for dependent care, adoption assistance, flexible spending accounts, domestic partner benefits, child care centers, family day care networks, emergency child care, preschool programs, after school programs, training and support groups, dependent care resource and referral, relocation assistance, and elder care programs.

Implementation of work-family programs is often the first step in a company's development of programs to attract, retain, develop, and advance women. Such programs are fundamental to women's retention and upward mobility, since most women in the U.S. labor force are in their prime childbearing years.

The impact of work-family programs on measurable phenomena such as absenteeism and tardiness and retention are clear. A 1990 study by the Urban Institute showed that 35 percent of mothers with children under twelve years old had a sick child in the last month; 51 percent of them missed work to care for their sick child. A 1987 *Fortune Magazine* study reported that 25 percent of employees with children under twelve years old experienced child care breakdowns two to five times in a three-month period.

Breakdowns were linked to higher absenteeism and tardiness, as well as lower concentration on the job and less marital and parental satisfaction. Aetna increased its retention rate for women from 77 percent to 88 percent when it instituted a six-month leave program with flexible return-to-work possibilities. Based on a cost-of-turnover study (Galinsky, 1993) that found employee replacement costs 193 percent of annual salary, Aetna estimates its savings to be $1 million per year.

A positive impact of work-family programs on less easily measured factors such as productivity, morale, and loyalty has also been suggested by responses to opinion surveys: six studies have found lower absenteeism and improved productivity to be the most important benefits reported by employees who were surveyed (Conference Board, 1991). Eight studies of manager perceptions of the impact of child care assistance found the major benefits were better morale and lower absenteeism (Conference Board, 1991). A large study that examined corporate responses to maternity found pregnant employees who worked for more family-responsive companies were more satisfied with their jobs, felt sick less often, missed less work, spent more uncompensated time working, worked later in their pregnancies, and were more likely to return to their jobs (National Council of Jewish Women, 1987, 1993).

While work-family programs are necessary and fundamental steps for companies that are concerned about recruitment, retention, development, and advancement of women, they are not sufficient to guarantee women's career advancement, nor are they universally applicable: women with children do not all have the same level of need for corporate-sponsored work-family benefits, and neither do women who never had children.

Catalyst does find that more and more American companies and firms are discovering that flexibility helps them retain experienced employees and attract the best group of new employees. They recognize that a flexible environment can help them serve global customers, meet cyclical or seasonal business needs, provide continuity on projects, and deliver more effective client service.

The twenty years of Catalyst research on flexibility shows that it is central to the recruitment, retention, and advancement of women, supporting women and men at critical times in their lives and benefiting the employer as well. Catalyst's handbook *Making Work Flexible: Policy to Practice* lays out the building blocks for a flexible work environment, as illustrated in Exhibit II.1.

Corporate best practices in the area of work-life balance run the gamut from child care centers to leaves for elder care to flextime (altering the hours at which one begins and ends the work day while maintaining an eight-hour schedule), part-time, job sharing (two employees jointly fulfill the responsibilities of one position) telecommuting and maternity leaves.

Women's Workplace Networks

Corporate women's networks provide an opportunity for management as well as a career development resource for women. Catalyst's research on these networks shows that there is no typical group; they vary in terms of membership, structure, and reason for origin. However, most share the same basic goals of encouraging women's professional business objectives. Most groups focus on career and skills development, promotion of networking, and improvement of communication between women and management, or some combination of these activities. Some extend their scope to examine corporate policy issues such as career mobility, managing diversity, and child care. Groups pursue their objectives through a variety of channels, such as speaking engagements, workshops, task forces, and published reports.

Gender Awareness Training and Safety Training

A 1996 article in *Across the Board* pegged the amount companies invest in training at over $30 billion annually. Historically, most training by companies has focused on skills development or enhancement

Exhibit II.1. Building Blocks for a Flexible Work Environment

Goals	Strategies			
Build Organizational Support	Define and explain link to business goals	Ensure and communicate senior management support	Articulate commitment to flexibility	Identify and support pilot programs
Support Managers and Employees	Provide tools	Evaluate effectiveness	Share models and case studies	If necessary, revise systems
Internalize the Practice	Incorporate into other initiatives	Create and support relationships and networks	Expand and refine HR department roles	Assess perceptions, experiences, and acceptance
Sustain the Commitment	Communicate internally about the issues	Promote flexibility externally	Implement account-ability measures	Evaluate work environment and modify activities

related to production and sales of products and services. Today, companies also provide a range of training opportunities focused on interpersonal competencies like communication and conflict resolution and on human resources management activities such as recruiting, coaching and performance appraisal, and feedback. And manager training is critical to effective implementation, utilization, and evaluation of diversity initiatives.

Training has become increasingly important in companies that are downsizing and restructuring, where a smaller employee base requires a broader skill set. In addition to the original purpose of skills building, training today is used to build teams, change cultures, and communicate company values. Most companies with which Catalyst is familiar have embarked on some form of training around gender awareness and broader diversity awareness programs, as well as activities more focused on sexual harassment or work-life conflicts of employees.

Many companies initially seek outside assistance in undertaking some form of diversity training. Train-the-trainer programs have been used by companies such as Allstate and Stentor to develop an internal group of trainers whose job it is to reinforce initial learning, identify new training needs, and ensure that new hires are brought up to speed on the company's diversity values and goals.

The costs of training are known and expressed in dollars, but the benefits are harder to measure. Many companies fail to measure the results of diversity training through the use of hard data (recruitment and retention numbers, for example) or softer performance areas that can be measured through surveys, focus groups, and individual interviews. Changing attitudes about diversity takes longer than changing specific behaviors. Companies need to work on both fronts and recognize the difficulty of change in this area of corporate culture.

Training is only one of many components of successful women's advancement initiatives in companies that Catalyst has benchmarked. Yet many companies' diversity efforts and dollars are singularly focused on diversity training.

Catalyst's experience shows that training is a necessary component of successful corporate leadership development initiatives, but does not suffice as a stand-alone approach to individual and organizational growth. More and more corporations and firms are including training as part of their overall initiatives to recruit, retain, and advance women. These vary from sexual harassment training and gender awareness training to programs to enhance safety.

References

Conference Board. *Linking Work-Family Issues to the Bottom Line*. New York: Conference Board, 1991.

Galinsky, E. *Thirteen Consistent (and Sometimes Surprising) Findings from Work-Family Evaluations*. Unpublished manuscript. New York: Families and Work Institute, 1993.

National Council of Jewish Women. *Accommodating Pregnancy in the Workplace*. New York: National Council of Jewish Women, 1987.

National Council of Jewish Women. *Experience of Childbearing Women in the Workplace: The Impact of Family-Friendly Policies and Practices*. New York: National Council of Jewish Women, 1993.

Benchmarking Culture

■■■

TEXAS INSTRUMENTS

Electronics

Headquarters: Dallas

Employees: 42,000

Annual revenues: $10 billion

Catalyst Award: 1996

Teaming Up for Achievement

Texas Instruments (TI), an international technology company, is the world's leader in digital signal processing solutions. Products and services include semiconductors, calculators, and digital imaging. The company invented the first integrated circuit.

The Initiative

The Texas Instruments philosophy, *"teaming is how we do business,"* originated in 1989 on the assembly line, where a work team managed to cut cycle times and improve customer satisfaction. Gradually, teaming became a new way to solve problems in other areas. After a business division won the Baldrige Award in 1992, TI adopted the team approach for the entire company. The goals of the initiative were

- An inclusive environment and culture

- Diversity at all levels

- Individual responsibility for growth, learning, and excellence

The team approach is particularly appropriate for pursuing diversity objectives: teaming involves getting people from different functions, with different expertise and different levels of authority, to work together purposefully. Learning to work together in that context, the company believes, is similar to learning to work with people of different backgrounds, who have different types of cultural knowledge or experience.

Women have much to gain in the culture of teams at TI, where lower-level employees are given access to senior-level mentors and role models. Furthermore, women who were once isolated are able to connect with women in other parts of the organization. Through teaming, less experienced employees have exposure to managers from different areas and higher levels, creating opportunities for networking and sharing information. This translates into increased visibility for women and people of color. The increased visibility of women encourages managers to take risks on other women.

Teams exist at all levels of TI. At the highest level, Strategic Leadership Teams create a network of teams different from the traditional hierarchy. This team includes the CEO and TI's senior officers. Within each group, there are various support function leadership teams. There are also teams that lead business priorities, such as the Leadership Development Process, and there are work teams in production areas carrying out work processes. Many teams include TI people from all around the world.

Teams are formed in two ways: by appointment or by choice. Managers can appoint people to teams to create solutions or drive a process. Employees can create teams voluntarily, if they identify an opportunity or need that can be addressed by a team. Women and minorities are included on teams, as TI believes that diversity of thought enhances business transactions.

Communication

The Teaming and Measurement initiative targets forty-two thousand employees worldwide, including twenty thousand U.S. employees. Communication about teaming begins in recruitment. TI uses a number of mechanisms to communicate information internally, including department meetings, newsletters, e-mail, brochures, brown bag lunch forums, coffee talks with the executives, regular team meetings, and day-to-day business gatherings. In addition, TI's grassroots employee diversity initiative uses the team approach to accelerate the progress of diversity across the corporation.

Impact

An increased visibility of women was the greatest quantitative result. Teaming supports inclusion, which also reduces the chance that women will be left out of networks. Workforce statistics show that the proportion of women in managerial and executive positions increased as the total number of managerial positions was reduced. From the end of 1989 to 1997, the number of women who work in management and team leadership positions at the entry level and above has doubled. Women and minorities serve in TI's network of leadership teams. Last year two women were named as officers in Asia, which the company says is very significant because it has very few vice presidents.

Key Elements

- Development of communication and work mechanism (teams) to create an inclusive culture

- Clearly defined targets and goals

- An effective measurement tool for assessing progress

- Integration of a personal development program into the initiative

STENTOR RESOURCE CENTRE, INC.

Telecommunications

Headquarters: Ottawa, Ontario, Canada

Culture Change

Stentor Resource Centre, Inc. (SRCI) was created in 1993 to pool all marketing, engineering, and product development capabilities of all the major provincial telephone companies in Canada, Stentor Owner Companies (also known as the Stentor Alliance). SRCI works with the Alliance to bring products and services to market. Although SRCI is only a few years old, most employees, including many senior managers, came from Bell Canada, the largest of the Canadian phone companies; the average employee tenure with a telephone company is twenty years.

SRCI implemented the systemic-level change initiative, Creating the Future, to support and enhance a reengineering process catalyzed by poor customer service ratings and with the mission to change the organization's culture from what senior managers called "hierarchical, process-oriented, complaining, and negative."

The Initiative

Conceived, designed, led, and implemented by women, with the support of the president-champion and the aid of outside consultants, Creating the Future focused on developing techniques all managers could use to improve their skills. One consequence was a companywide recognition that many women have the skills needed for leadership. Seventy percent of the 1176 managers were men, and SRCI points out that turning over leadership for this culture change to women managers was a first for the company.

The main vehicle of the initiative was a three-day workshop for project teams, which involved participation by the SRCI senior leadership team and by customers, as well as precourse consultation with team leaders and individuals attending the workshops, and coaching following the workshops to provide support for the teams in realizing the new projects created at the workshops. The first stage involved equipping SRCI individuals to lead the organization-wide workshops and sustain the cultural change effort. Once rolled out, there were three workshops per week during a nine-month period, and fifteen hundred SRCI employees attended the workshops.

Communication

The workshops emphasized communication, and the company found the result was an open dialogue between project team members, customers, and upper management. The program used several methods to communicate to the organization, including the "Express," a biweekly bulletin to all employees that devoted one issue to the program and included a message from the CEO regarding culture change. There were also Town Hall meetings with employees, voice mail messages from the CEO, and a Lotus Notes data base for sharing success stories.

Accountability

The SRCI Executive Team made an up-front commitment to the Creating the Future project and the team held itself accountable for meeting the timeline. Team members also actively participated in the workshops prior to their roll-out to the entire employee body. The CEO championed the initiative.

Impact

The visibility of women in running the workshops led to a change in the perception about women's leadership and risk-taking capability; the new CEO appointed since the initiative is a woman, and women report that gender is no longer the issue it once was at

SRCI. The company reports that customer satisfaction improved by 25 percent over a six-month period. In this new culture, flexibility has been implemented throughout; many people telecommute and a generous maternity leave is offered, with women returning without penalty even after as much as a year's leave.

Key Elements

- Initiative designed and implemented by women in middle management

- Entire employee population participated in workshops

- CEO as champion

- Executive team accountable

DELOITTE & TOUCHE

Accounting and auditing, tax, and management consulting

Headquarters: Wilton, Connecticut

Employees: 23,000

Annual revenues: $3.66 billion

Catalyst Award: 1995

Initiative for the Retention and Advancement of Women

Deloitte & Touche, which spends nearly $1 billion a year on the recruitment and training of its people, sees the departure of high-talent professionals as a blow to productivity and customer-service continuity. The disproportionately high turnover rate among women professionals led Deloitte & Touche in January 1992 to target retention and advancement of high-talent women as "a business imperative for the 1990s."

The Program

D&T's initiative has several interrelated pieces. Among the most important:

- *Support from the top:* J. Michael Cook, Deloitte & Touche's chairman and CEO, has taken an active role in championing the Initiative.

- *Open dialogue:* In "Men and Women as Colleagues" seminars, D&T partners and managers have been able to discuss challenges and opportunities presented by the initiative. Both men and women report that after the workshops, they feel much freer to raise issues, especially gender issues, that concern them.

- *Careful tracking of assignments:* Deloitte & Touche is careful to make sure women are getting an equitable share of the challenging or high-profile assignments.

- *Flexible work arrangements:* Deloitte & Touche offers a range of options, including flextime, reduced workload, and telecommuting.

- *Career development:* With the initiative, the firm instituted a policy of having written three-to-five-year career development plans for female senior managers and partners.

- *Women's Initiative Network (WIN):* Sixty partners across the country were chosen for their stature and commitment to the initiative. The network was created to make certain the initiative took root throughout Deloitte and Touche's network of individual offices. Each office is responsible for developing a plan of action related to the initiative and has the latitude to determine the types of activities most likely to produce desired results.

Accountability

Both national and local human resources professionals, along with WIN leaders, monitor efforts on the initiative. WIN leaders, all of whom are client service partners, spend 10 percent to 20 percent of their time on the initiative. In addition to the network, the firm established the Council on the Advancement of Women, chaired by former Secretary of Labor Lynn Martin and consisting of distinguished independent professionals who have made significant contributions to issues affecting women. The council is responsible for advising firm leaders on the best methods of achieving their goals, for providing objective oversight, and for ensuring meaningful progress by monitoring, measuring, motivating, and keeping the firm focused on its goals. Putting himself and the firm on the line by going public with this initiative, the chairman and chief executive bears ultimate responsibility for implementation and accountability.

Communication

Chairman and CEO Mike Cook has invested a great deal of his time and the firm's financial and human resources to ensure the success of the Initiative for the Retention and Advancement of Women. He has been interviewed extensively by print and broadcast media and has spoken across the country at numerous events. This visible senior management commitment has proved critical to the initiative's success. In addition, recognizing that success would depend not only on buy-in at the very top but also on the understanding and support of all professionals within the firm, Deloitte & Touche has used newsletters, letters from top management, partner meetings, videos, press conferences and interviews with media, and other public forums and speaking platforms to communicate the rationale for the initiative, its progress, firm goals, and plans for implementation.

Impact

Since the implementation of the initiative, the percentage of women admitted to partnership has increased from 8 percent in 1991 to 20 percent in 1997. Women partners now account for 10 percent of all partners, up from 5 percent in 1991. In addition, the gap in turnover rate between men and women has narrowed, particularly at the higher levels (partner, senior manager, manager). Over seven hundred professionals take advantage of flexible work arrangements today, including fifteen partners. The firm has tripled the number of women in key leadership positions since 1993.

Key Elements

- Chief executive as champion, visible internally and externally

- Partner buy-in

- Equitable share of important clients assigned to women

- Advancement possible while using flexibility options

BANK OF MONTREAL

Chartered bank

Employees: 34,826

Average assets: $147 billion

Catalyst Award: 1994

Debunking the Myths

In the early 1990s, as part of a shift in the Bank of Montreal's strategic direction to become "the bank of choice for employees," it undertook a gender initiative, believing that addressing women's issues was the first step toward a sweeping change in the culture. The bank looked at basic demographics: although women made up at least 75 percent of the bank's employee population, they were only 9 percent of the executive ranks.

The Initiative

In 1991, F. Anthony Comper, the bank's president and CEO, commissioned the Task Force on the Advancement of Women to identify the barriers to women's advancement and recommend measures to eradicate them. The bank committed $1 million to the task force for nine months of activity. When the task force met resistance, the bank released an executive report on the critical nature of women's advancement to the new corporate strategic plan and emphasized broadening the talent pool.

The task force, headed by a woman with extensive line experience, had four full-time and eleven part-time members representing the bank demographically—75 percent women, 25 percent men—regionally, and by division; all became ambassadors of the group's work. A steering committee and consultative group provided support for the task force's work, also speaking out on task force findings. The task force benchmarked externally against forty-three companies with model programs. To begin internal benchmarking, they met with thirty-five hundred bankers in a total of 185 meetings.

Then, with the help of outside consultants, they interviewed 270 bank employees and held eleven focus groups. From these the task force learned about myths that prevailed at the organization regarding women. These were confirmed by a survey that went out to over fifteen thousand people in the bank—with over ninety-five hundred responses—and an alumni survey that went to two thousand former employees. The research identified five main commonly held beliefs as to why so few women had reached senior positions at the bank (see Chapter Two); the task force analyzed the facts about the twenty-eight thousand full- and part-time employees stored in the Human Resources Information System to test those assumptions. They found that women had equaled or surpassed their male colleagues in education, length of service, dedication, and job performance. They also learned that another assumption was false, that women would advance at the bank, given time; at the rate women were advancing in 1991, they would still make up only 18 percent of executive ranks by 2000. The bank continued its myth-busting process with a follow-up study. It countered a new myth that men would now not be promoted by showing the stats: that men made up 62 percent of all promotions to senior management that year.

The task force called for the creation of a new department, Workplace Equality, responsible for implementing its recommendations and for ensuring a fully integrated approach to cultural change within the bank. The Workplace Equality team oversaw various initiatives, including gender awareness workshops, flexible work arrangements, child care, elder care, the revision of policies to support and reflect diversity and equality perspectives, a national career information network, and an executive adviser program.

Communication

The bank distributed its reports to over a thousand outside organizations.

Accountability

The Task Force monitored the annual business plan process in which eleven managers set goals for hiring, retaining, and advancing women and people of color and for the quarterly performance review process, ensuring accountability. The team approached tracking through a variety of channels, including employee feedback compiled in a report to the chief operating officer.

Impact

Women at the organization felt that the strength of the Task Force's recommendations lay in their application to men as well as women, and that the resulting initiatives would lead to changes for both genders. Between October 1991 and October 1997, the representation of women in executive positions increased from 9 percent to 50 percent. Of particular interest, representation at senior vice president level increased from 3 to 27 percent, and representation within senior management positions has increased from 13 to 26 percent.

Key Elements

- Elaborate research process supporting a solid business case to motivate managers

- Integration into the business organization

- Supervision by president rather than Human Resources

PRICE WATERHOUSE

Accounting and consulting

Headquarters: New York

Employees: 16,000 (U.S.)

Annual revenues: $5.6 billion

New Career Model

Like other large accounting and consulting firms, Price Waterhouse
has experienced a high turnover rate, yet it is poised to grow. The
firm reports that women in particular were leaving for two reasons:
its lack of flexibility and inability to either slow or speed up career
progression. To deal with these and other related issues, the firm developed a new career model that reduces what it calls the "cultural
rigidity that works counter to business." Such a new model, the firm
believed, would draw the best talent into the firm, as well as allow it
to develop those individuals and leverage their intellectual capital.
The new, more flexible career structure also meant incorporating
new evaluation and compensation systems.

The Initiative

Under Price Waterhouse's previous system, people were classified as
staff, manager, senior manager, or partner. The partnership track
generally meant an individual's spending three years at each level,
working full time and being measured against same-year hires. People moved along according to the firm's plan and went elsewhere if
they didn't make partner or were not perceived as partner material;
this is known informally as the *up-or-out* model.

The new career model dismantles the up-or-out system, focusing on competencies and allowing individuals to progress at their
own pace, including developing a particular expertise. A career thus
may both fit individual needs and the needs of clients who demand
deep skill sets. Each individual is paired with a coach who helps the

professional map out a career development plan. The professional communicates what skill sets she has and what kinds of developmental opportunities she would like, and the coach shares the information with the resource manager. The firm overhauled its salary bands and evaluation process to support the new system, so that compensation reflects what the marketplace pays for particular skills.

In addition, Price Waterhouse has adopted a formal process for assigning engagements. When a new client comes in, the project manager of the new engagement goes to the resource manager for staffing, specifying the skills needed. The resource manager goes through the database of information all professionals have provided and matches individuals with engagements.

The firm also evolved programs that help support the new career model, including

- *Mentoring circles:* Senior women and men formally mentor in some regions of the country. A female and male partner are assigned a group of eight to twelve women.

- *Partnership Admission Committee:* The records of women who do not make partner are scrutinized carefully for evidence of discrimination. People who do not make partner are offered career development coaching.

Communication

The flexible work arrangements program is used in recruitment. It is also communicated through in-house periodicals and mentioned in all formal literature. Price Waterhouse communicates about the program in these ways as well:

- Peer discussion leaders talk informally to colleagues about the model.

- Using a Lotus Notes database, staff can ask questions anonymously.

- The firm circulates letters from top leadership, quarterly status reports, announcements, and press clips.

- It sponsors day-long regional information sessions.

- It shares success stories through local and firmwide newsletters.

Accountability

Practice leaders are evaluated and tracked on the level of diversity in their group. The firm keeps records of every major client assignment, including whether women were considered for key roles on the team.

Impact

The firm first rolled this model out in the consulting division in 1993 and early 1994. At the end of the implementation process for the consulting division, employees evaluated the process against objectives and made appropriate adjustments prior to rolling the program out in Europe. They have now adapted the career structures process to their tax, corporate finance, and accounting divisions, which have also been historically hierarchical, rigid, lockstep, and dependent on an up-or-out structure.

Price Waterhouse reports that the major challenge was dealing with perceptions of loss of status that resulted from the flattened hierarchy and the elimination of titles. The firm found it needed to address individual experiences during the roll-out process.

Before the new model, women with children generally had the perception that they did not have an equal chance to advance if they worked a reduced schedule. The new career model dispels that perception: it lets people feel comfortable culturally about working a reduced schedule. In fact, three women were recently admitted to partnership while they were working a reduced schedule. Flexibility allows people to progress at their own pace. Turnover among women in management has been reduced by 10 percent. Overall turnover is down 25 percent. The number of female partners has increased by 23 percent. When Price Waterhouse surveyed staff opinion about the initiative, 92 percent expressed a positive view.

Key Element

- The model is seen as a way to improve business performance rather than a Human Resources project

SARA LEE CORPORATION

Consumer products

Headquarters: Chicago, Illinois

Employees: 141,000 worldwide

Annual revenues: $19.7 billion

Strategic Diversity: A Business Imperative

Sara Lee, the maker and marketer of food and other consumer products, states clearly that it has a special responsibility to encourage and advance women: the majority of its workforce is female and women are by far the most frequent purchasers of Sara Lee products. In the early 1990s, Sara Lee began developing the long-range strategic diversity plan that eventually became the Balanced Workforce Initiative, a program of eight strategically focused initiatives designed to help the corporation recruit, develop, value, work with, and maintain a diverse culture. The Strategic Diversity initiative includes communications, management accountability, organizational policies and practices, balanced workforce, quality of life, global focus, training and development, and sponsorship and community support.

The Strategic Diversity initiative focuses on goals to increase the representation of women and minorities at management levels of the organization. The goals were established by considering demographic statistics, the profiles of the customers who use Sara Lee products, and the profiles of those who make the purchasing decisions for Sara Lee products.

Sara Lee is a diverse corporation made up of many autonomous business units. The corporate office develops diversity strategies and goals and presents them to the Employee and Public Responsibility Committee, the largest standing committee of Sara Lee's board of directors, on an annual basis for review and approval. The goals are then communicated to the business units. While the overall diversity strategies and annual goals are developed at the corporate level, each division actually drives its diversity process independently. The corporate strategies are used as guidelines in determining individual implementation plans based on the division's culture and organizational needs.

Sara Lee's leadership is committed to identifying and developing women to fill key management positions. Sara Lee uses an internal succession planning review process to spot and track employees who have the potential to move quickly up the ladder at the company. Department heads recommend employees for the high-potential list and ensure that they get training in the skills necessary to advance as envisioned. Within succession planning, a specific review is completed of high-potential women and minorities. The review is held annually in all Sara Lee divisions.

Communication

The leadership of Sara Lee communicates its diversity and management development strategies, goals, and initiatives in a variety of ways as diverse as its workforce. Chairman and CEO John Bryan is highly visible and vocal regarding the company's balanced workforce initiatives; he drives support of women's initiatives through speeches given both internally and externally, and through written directives to the senior management team and division operating management of the corporation. He also demonstrates his personal and corporate commitment through involvement and sponsorship of organizations and events that drive women's initiatives. The senior management team drives communication of goals and the ongoing management development through the quarterly business reviews, the dedication of bonus standards to diversity and management development initiatives and the annual succession planning review process.

In addition, a review of the female and minority diversity and development goals, results, and initiatives is presented to the Sara Lee board of directors periodically throughout the year.

The corporation and its divisions use multiple communication media to reinforce the commitment and communicate initiatives and results of the balanced workforce initiatives. Initiatives and results are included in recruitment materials, business review plans, newsletters, various ads in magazines, sponsorship of events, internal roundtables, leadership forums and task forces, and best practice sessions.

Accountability

Goal setting and communication of goals and results are an integral part of the Sara Lee culture, and the company plans to measure this initiative against goals in the same way it measures financial performance against goals. This is sometimes described as "What gets measured, gets done." In support of the Strategic Diversity initiative, Sara Lee established a goal that 40 percent of the 1996 MBA hires would be women. By starting out with a diverse base of management employees, Sara Lee hopes to achieve a competitive edge in developing women directors, vice presidents, divisional presidents, and corporate officers. Another aggressive goal of the Strategic Diversity initiative is to ensure that 30 percent of the women who are identified as high-potentials are promoted or moved laterally for development each year. In addition, an aggressive set of representation goals is established by business groups. These and other diversity initiatives are included in the annual bonus standards for all Sara Lee presidents. Since achieving goals is important to the Sara Lee culture, including diversity as a measure in the bonus standards demonstrates Sara Lee's commitment to this process.

In addition to setting annual goals, John Bryan (the chairman and chief executive) and the two executive vice presidents, along with the president and chief operating officer and the vice chairman of the corporation, have been vocally supportive of the diversity initiatives and have endorsed them in written communication to their direct reports. They have recently put into place plans to monitor diversity quarterly during their business updates. Diversity is also included on the agenda at the annual President's Conference.

Impact

There are now 163 women in key assignments—one-quarter of the total—throughout Sara Lee.

The company also sponsors events and activities oriented to women:

- Sara Lee gives the Frontrunner Award annually to honor four women for outstanding contributions to their fields: the arts, business, government, and the humanities.

- The company commissioned an opinion poll last year to learn about women's perspectives on work and family life.

- Sara Lee hosts the Sara Lee Classic, a fifty-four-hole golf tournament on the Ladies Professional Golf Association tour.

- Sara Lee sponsors women's roundtables, which provide a forum for women leaders to analyze current sociological trends and practices.

Key Elements

- CEO as champion

- Setting percentage goals

- President's bonus tied to achieving goals

PITNEY BOWES, INC.

Messaging products and services

Headquarters: Stamford, Connecticut

Employees: 32,792

Annual revenues: $3.9 billion

Catalyst Award: 1994

Diversity Strategic Plan

Pitney Bowes is made up of ten business units that provide products and services to help companies address all their messaging needs. In 1992, the company initiated a process to formalize its long-standing commitment to valuing a diverse work force. A task force was formed to draft a diversity vision statement and create a strategic plan that would serve as a model for each business unit.

The twenty-four members of the task force were diverse in terms of job functions and level, as well as in terms of race, age, gender, ethnicity, and sexual orientation. Representatives from the Minorities and Women's Resource groups were included to ensure the representation of their respective issues in the strategic plan.

The Plan

The task force's strategy served as a foundation from which each business unit wrote individualized plans incorporating such actions as mentoring, rotational and special assignments, preparing competency models for management positions, strengthening the employee career planning process, conducting and analyzing exit interviews, and including a diversity component in orientation and manager training. While the focus of these plans is on women and other diverse groups, the overall Diversity Strategic Plan affirms a commitment to create a culture that fosters the development and upward mobility of all Pitney Bowes employees.

Each business unit's progress in carrying out its diversity strategies is measured in meetings with the chairman and all business unit heads. The company's commitment to diversity as a competitive imperative is underscored by the practice of tying each business unit head's bonus with their unit's year-end diversity results rating.

Communication

Part of the success of the diversity strategy is open communication. Each business unit's diversity strategy has a communication component that results in a wide variety of activities such as seminars, diversity newsletters, and multicultural fairs. Employees have been kept apprised of the goals and results of the diversity strategic plans through employee publications in each business unit and in *PB Today*, the corporate publication. The company also regularly communicates with employees about diversity as a business imperative.

Impact

By implementing the Diversity Strategic Plan, Pitney Bowes has strongly affirmed that developing and maintaining a diverse workforce is an essential business practice. And its success is evident— the number of women in management has increased steadily over the past several years. The current results are impressive:

- Twenty percent of senior management (director-level and above) are women.

- Eighteen percent of the board of directors are women.

- Thirty-six percent of the corporate officers are women.

Key Elements

- Business units create individualized plans

- Accountability to chairman and business unit heads

- Bonuses of business unit heads tied to diversity rating

HOECHST CELANESE CORPORATION

Chemicals

Headquarters: Bridgewater, New Jersey

Employees: 29,900

Annual revenues: $6.9 billion

Catalyst Award: 1996

Vertical Parity Initiative

Hoechst Celanese Corporation is a science-based, market-driven international company that produces and markets chemicals, fibers, plastics, polyester film, printing plates, dyes and pigments, pharmaceuticals, animal-health and crop-protection products, and other high-performance advanced materials.

The Initiative

Hoechst Celanese Corporation created its Vertical Parity Initiative in response to 1992 projections on the changing demographics of its workforce. Its goal is to represent women and people of color at all levels in numbers mirroring the workforce from which the company recruits. The company considers itself a "Preferred Employer" and its management recognized that in order to maintain this position, they would need to "further develop an environment in which women and minorities could thrive both professionally and personally."

The initiative was designed primarily to measure progress and to provide overall direction to addressing any barriers to the progress of women and minorities to management and decision-making positions. The initiative includes a range of programs, including diversity training, mentoring, succession planning, tools for individual career design, and a system for early identification of high-potential women.

The Operating Committee measures progress toward diversity goals. No specific programs are mandated by the Operating Committee, so that business groups may create their own initiatives as appropriate to their environments.

The diversity training programs are designed to enhance the awareness and understanding of individual differences and to avoid stereotyping. The program began with the CEO and 150 senior managers. Each participated in sessions that sought to explore personal biases and stereotypes. Diversity training evolved into all seven business groups, and corporate staff have initiated programs. All corporate employees completed one full day of training, which was designed to help participants develop an awareness and sensitivity to cultural, racial, and gender differences, and then a three-day workshop. This workshop focuses on helping employees begin to build the leadership and communications skills required to manage and work in a diverse workforce. The emphasis is on increasing the quality and sense of team required to function in the diverse workplace.

Communication

The company initially communicated the Vertical Parity Initiative through group level meetings, distribution of newsletters, e-mail, and a pamphlet summarizing the VPI along with a letter from the CEO emphasizing the importance of diversity (sent to each employee's home).

Accountability

Line managers, rather than Human Resources staff, have responsibility for diversity at Hoechst Celanese. Managers are evaluated on how they recruit and identify critical training needs and opportunities for their people. Managers review their work in these areas once a year with corporate Human Resources and twice a year with regional Human Resources. Achievement of diversity goals accounts for 25 percent of management bonuses. Managers are held accountable at the departmental and group level. Progress on parity and diversity goals is also measured by the Operating Committee (made up of senior managers). Hoechst Celanese has prepared managers to be accountable for the success of the diversity initiatives by presenting a diversity summary to middle managers—a tool to teach managers how to be accountable and reach their diversity goals. This same summary will be rolled out to entry-level managers in the near future.

Measurement Goals

The project began with development of Group level plans—Five and Ten Year Equality Plans, for 1996 and 2001 respectively, with goals that business groups must reach. Group plans were subsequently rolled up into a single corporate plan. The projections for the plans are very specific. The projections are to increase representation of women at Hoechst Celanese to 29 percent by year-end 2001. The progress is measured quarterly by the senior management group.

Impact

The Vertical Parity Initiative has already yielded measurable results: from 1991 to 1995, the number of women in senior management increased 20 percent.

Key Elements

- Clear understanding of the link between the goals of the initiative and the company's business plan

- Line management responsibility for progress toward goals, as would be true for any business initiative

- Clear, measurable goals

- Regular evaluation of progress toward those goals

ALLSTATE CORPORATION

Insurance

Headquarters: Northbrook, Illinois

Employees: 45,898

Annual revenues: $24.3 billion

Catalyst Award: 1997

Creating an Environment for Success: Diversity Index

Allstate is the second-largest insurer of automobiles and homes in the United States, as well as a marketer of commercial insurance. It was spun off from its parent, Sears Roebuck and Company, in 1993. Although the company was once regarded as insular—much like the insurance industry itself—it now has a reputation as something of a maverick. It has informally favored diversity for many years; more recently it formalized diversity as a corporate strategy by adopting its "Creating an Environment for Success" initiative, which is meant to open up opportunities for all employees, for their advancement and the company's benefit.

The Practice

With one piece of its diversity initiative, Allstate has taken a great leap forward in measurement and accountability. The company developed an on-line questionnaire, the Quarterly Leadership Measurement System (QLMS), which all employees answer anonymously four times a year.

The diversity index, a subset of the QLMS survey, and the company's skills-based diversity education curriculum, are the two most notable aspects of its overall initiative. The survey, begun in 1995, is part of a still broader system designed to measure customer satisfaction, shareholder value, process effectiveness, and employee effectiveness. Diversity is one of three components of employee effectiveness. Within the broader survey of effectiveness, Allstate poses such questions as: "Does the company deliver quality service to customers regardless of ethnic background?" "How often do you observe insensitive behavior at work, e.g., jokes about ethnic backgrounds or inappropriate remarks?" "Does your immediate manager/ team leader utilize different backgrounds and perspectives?" From the answers to these and other questions, the company created the diversity index, which it uses to develop action plans and goals for annual improvement.

Communication

Allstate views diversity as a strategy to help it achieve its business goals; it integrates the diversity message into all communications about the company. Internally, the company communicates via published measurement results and articles in company publications like its various diversity newsletters. Face-to-face communication includes quarterly town hall meetings, senior management team diversity sessions, diversity team presentations, and feedback for all senior management.

Accountability

Survey responses are printed out so that leaders get feedback on how they are doing—and Allstate gets an indication of how its leadership is doing. The diversity index is tied to incentive compensation for bonuses. Leaders are accountable; pay and promotion are affected and the index signals to the Allstate workforce that the company's leadership is serious about diversity.

Impact

The initiative has not yet been evaluated quantitatively, but employees report that the beginning of a fundamental culture change is under way. Talented women are given greater responsibility, training, recognition, and promotion; inroads have been made into traditionally male-dominated departments, and in other areas of the business, the opportunities for women are increasing.

Key Elements

- Workforce-wide survey includes diversity questions
- Survey's diversity results linked to managers' bonuses

AVON MEXICO

Cosmetics

Headquarters: Mexico City

Employees: 3,000

Annual revenues: $297.5 million

Catalyst Award: 1997

Living a Vision for Women

Avon Mexico is the Mexican unit of the big New York–based cosmetics products corporation, Avon, Inc., which for years has supported developing and advancing women and won the Catalyst Award for its 1988 initiative "Communication System for Managing Workplace Diversity." The initiative at Avon Mexico began with its recent redefinition of its vision: "To be the company that best understands and satisfies the product, service and self-fulfillment needs of women globally." Avon Mexico not only stresses creating career opportunities for women and a culture where women can be successful, but also supports a broad range of women's interests in Mexico, including breast cancer research plus women's athletics, academic scholarships, and cultural activities.

The Initiative

The full initiative grew out of explorations by the task force set up to investigate the climate for women at Avon Mexico. The team used surveys, interviews, and workshops incorporating men and women at all levels throughout the organization.

The workshops were the centerpiece of the exploration. They examined how men and women work together, how they want to be treated, and what expectations they have of the company. From these workshops came suggestions on linking the vision with new approaches to strategic orientation, decision making, career planning, leadership development, and work environment. The suggestions were bundled into a report formulating the collective vision.

The emphasis on men and women working together has made an impact on the day-to-day culture at Avon Mexico. The chief executive continues to champion the initiative with clients and employees. Employees view the initiative as a motivational tool and believe it has changed Avon's average Mexican company image to one of a more focused, dynamic, responsive company.

In response to concerns raised in the workshops and surveys, Avon has created a range of career development programs for all employees, including:

- Training programs in various communication and personal growth skills

- A personal development program devised by the employee, a supervisor, and the Human Resources department to help with career development

- A program to identify and develop high-potential talent

Communication

Articles about the initiative and vision appear regularly in company publications. Avon also sponsors a lecture series on female empowerment, for which the company brings in outside experts. Avon also sponsors a "Week of the Woman" every year by having a week of special events geared toward women.

One crucial outside part of the initiative is Avon Mexico's involvement in the community. Like its parent company, it underwrites a "Crusade Against Breast Cancer," an educational effort on early detection. The crusade provides mammography equipment for rural areas. Avon's Zazil Award is given annually to outstanding women in science, the arts, social action, and enterprise.

Accountability

Avon Mexico participates in an annual executive resources review at Avon Headquarters in New York, where Avon's top brass identify the executives with the highest potential for development and advancement. The system provides a rigorous review of the progress of the initiative. Human Resources reviews the profiles for each department against the profiles of high-potential employees to make sure the appropriate people are getting promotions.

Impact

In a country where women make up only 20 percent of the workforce, Avon Mexico stands out, with women comprising 54 percent of employees and 31 percent of managers within three reports of the president, up from 24 percent in 1993. Women represent 38 percent of employees assigned to strategic task forces and the company pays particular attention to staffing teams with both women and men. Avon Mexico's vice president for sales was Mexico's first woman vice president; she is still one of only a few in the country.

Key Element

- Integration into the overall culture of Avon Mexico

NABISCO FOOD GROUPS

Food

Headquarters: Parsippany, N.J.

Employees: 53,000

Annual Revenues: $8.3 billion

Compensation Equity

A number of practices at Nabisco Food Groups serve to ensure that gender-based pay inequities for sales representatives do not exist. Nabisco has a salary range for each job position; all employees in a particular position earn within that salary range. When Nabisco hires for the same job in the same region, it initially pays all employees the same salary.

Nabisco Food Groups has established a common review date for all representatives' performance ratings, which it determines by quantifiable measures that include the level of display activity, the introduction of new products, and customer satisfaction. Bonuses are based on this year's sales compared to last year's sales, thus eliminating any possible bias due to gender or race. Merit increases require multiple review levels; the employee's boss recommends performance ratings, which are reviewed and approved by the boss's boss and a Human Resources manager.

An annual companywide review of salaries provides an additional check for pay equity. Human Resources conducts an audit of all salaries within each salary grade and creates a spreadsheet to compare and contrast salaries of all employees in each salary grade by gender and by race. If a deviation in salary is found, Human Resources examines the employee records to see if the salary discrepancy can be explained by a legitimate difference in criteria, such as work experience or performance rating. Employees are urged to contact Human Resources if they believe there are compensation inequities. Human Resources can look into the allegation and either adjust the salary or explain the discrepancy.

Impact

Salary ranges limit disparities between employees in the same job. The multiple-level approval process ensures integrity and equity of performance ratings. In the same way, the three-tier approval process for salary increases ensures compensation equity, as no manager has carte blanche to reward or penalize employees.

Key Elements

- Salary ranges for job positions

- Bonus based on yearly comparison of sales figures

- Common review date

- Multiple approval levels

- Comparison of salaries

Women's Advancement

■■■

Recruitment

BOOZ ALLEN & HAMILTON, INC.

Management consulting

Headquarters: McLean, Virginia

Employees: 6,000 in the United States; 7,500 internationally

Annual revenues: $1.3 billion

Targeted Recruitment Program

After analyzing the acceptance rates of its MBA recruits, Booz Allen & Hamilton, the general management consulting firm, realized it had a gender gap in its new staff hires. Half its male recruits accepted offers, compared with less than a third of the female recruits. By benchmarking data on its competitors, Booz Allen found that the problem was not, as some proposed, that women simply were not choosing careers in consulting. Other consulting firms were successfully recruiting women. The firm decided to create a recruitment program targeted at women that it would run annually.

The Initiative

To reach out to women, Booz Allen held women-only dinners, with tables hosted by the firm's senior women, at its core eight business schools. From forty to a hundred people attended each event, depending on the size of the school.

The first year, a panel featured three successful female consultants who discussed their careers at Booz Allen and talked about issues of importance to women and their careers. Each table of ten discussed the issues and formulated recommendations for individuals and for organizations. The students' top three concerns were balancing work and personal life, communication between women and men at work, and mentoring. The moderator at each table kept notes, which were compiled into a report and sent to each guest after the event.

The second year, the event organizers used issues that had come up the previous year as a jumping-off point for the panel and table discussions. In subsequent years, they devised case studies to illustrate issues and stimulate discussion. The students seemed to view the dinners as a setting in which they could raise questions and discuss issues that they might not raise in an interview. The women from Booz Allen see the events as an opportunity to talk freely about issues that affect them at Booz Allen.

Impact

As indicated earlier, in 1994, 50 percent of male recruits accepted offers from the firm, compared with 30 percent of female recruits. In 1995, the first year of the initiative, 56 percent of the men accepted offers, and the number of women accepting jumped to 52 percent, a significant narrowing of the gender gap. In 1996, the gap was 5 percentage points: 53 percent of the men accepted, compared with 48 percent of the women.

The events have had an additional, unplanned networking benefit: it was the first time many of the women within the firm had met each other.

Key Element

- Emphasis on gender and work-life issues as legitimate business concerns, important for both men and women

CONSOLIDATED EDISON OF NEW YORK

Public utility

Headquarters: New York City

Employees: 15,200

Annual revenues: $6.9 million

Catalyst Award: 1988

Management Intern Program and Blue Collar Prep Program

Con Ed is one of the largest publicly owned gas and electric utili-
ties in the United States. The company provides power to more
than eight million people in most of New York City and Westchester County. It also supplies gas in Manhattan, the Bronx, and
parts of Queens and Westchester and steam in part of Manhattan.
It sells electricity to government customers through the New York
Power Authority.

Both the Management Intern Program and the support of the
Blue Collar Prep Program demonstrate Con Ed's dedication to the
advancement of women in nontraditional jobs. The Management
Intern Program allows recent college graduates the opportunity to
gain experience in their field. The Blue Collar Prep Program provides training and support for women who wish to enter traditionally male-dominated blue collar jobs. Con Ed received the Catalyst
Award in 1988.

Management Intern Program

Con Ed found that attracting women to a company where most
jobs require physical labor is a challenge. Motivated by changing
workforce demographics and a bottom-line concern to develop and
diversify management talent, Con Ed created a comprehensive
strategy called "Commitment to Women With Technical Talent."
The strategy was created to recruit, develop, and promote qualified
women. The centerpiece of this strategy is the Management Intern Program, which Con Ed launched in 1981. This program was

established for two reasons: to intensify efforts to recruit women, and to develop the future managers of the company.

In 1993, Con Ed divided the Management Intern Program into several organization-based programs:

- The Field Supervisory Intern Program for Engineers

- The Assistant Engineer Program

- The Gas Operation Management Development Program

- The Information Resources Assistant Computer Analyst Program

- The Business Intern Program, which is organization-wide

Another recent change is in the administration of the program. The Management Intern Program was once run solely by the College Programs Department. Now, the Recruitment and Staffing Department hires and places the interns, and Con Ed's Learning Center is responsible for the administration of the program. Mentors assist the director of the Learning Center by providing feedback to evaluate the effectiveness of its program.

The Programs

The programs generally recruit between ten and twenty college graduates annually. Managers conduct campus interviews with all potential candidates, who are assessed according to skills identified by the Competitive Skills Team. The managers in the recruiting and staffing department select candidates for the program. They are looking for technical competence, leadership potential, and communication skills. The Gas Operations Management and the Business Intern Programs both run for two years, while the Assistant Engineer and Field Supervisory Intern Programs take three years. Each program involves several short-term rotational assignments where the interns receive on-the-job supervision and mentoring from an assigned adviser.

After the first year, engineers go into a three-year rotation as first-line supervisors followed by three years in central operations. For interns who are not engineers, a one-year administrative training job follows the Management Intern Program. That year is spent in a field assignment in operations. These programs provide all participants with a range of experience and expose them to the field environment.

Each intern is assigned a mentor from mid- or upper-level management who is responsible for tracking the intern's progress. Managers meet regularly with interns to provide guidance and assistance. The assignments are evaluated by the Functional Review Committee, which is made up of senior-level managers and chaired by general managers. The program administrator is part of every review committee.

Accountability

When they complete the program, all graduates are expected to be well-rounded and able to fit into the department to which they are assigned. If the departments have a problem with a newly placed graduate, procedures call for them to tell the Learning Center. The program coordinator will be made aware of these problems and held accountable for the program's success. To date, there have been no reported problems from any of the departments.

Communication

The Management Intern Program is highlighted throughout company publications. Con Ed recruits for the program from among seniors at targeted colleges and universities and attends job fairs to publicize the program.

Impact

While women make up only 17 percent of engineering students nationally, they are more than 30 percent of the participants in the Management Intern Program. There has been a great demand for program graduates from departments. All graduates are placed into departments upon completion of the program.

Blue Collar Prep Program

Con Ed is a cosponsor of the Blue Collar Prep program, developed by Nontraditional Employment of Women (NEW), a nonprofit organization based in New York City. This program prepares women for nontraditional jobs educationally, psychologically, and physically through training. The program is financed by grants from government and private agencies.

Con Ed uses the Blue Collar Prep program to recruit women to work in nontraditional jobs, for example, as general utility workers. When a number of openings are available at the company, Con Ed will contact the Blue Collar Prep Program and recruit from its pool of qualified women. Con Ed provides funding, training instructors, and tools in support of the Blue Collar Prep program. Recruiting efforts vary according to the entry-level positions available.

The Program

The program focuses on helping women and their future managers address potential barriers to acceptance in the field. The women are trained in many different trades. The supervisors receive training on sensitivity and gender issues. During training the women are assigned mentors. Training is administered by NEW and varies according to the specific contract of funding. Length of time, targeted population, and expected achievement all vary with the contract. For example, training may be longer and made up of different elements, including basic reading and math skills, if a program is targeted to a low-educational-level population.

Since its beginning, collaboration with existing nonprofit organizations has been a successful recruiting strategy for Con Ed. The company has similar relationships with various other nonprofit training programs. When an organization has at least 30 percent female trainees or participants, Con Ed will work with the organization and recruit as many qualified candidates as possible. The recruiting efforts continuously work toward a fundamental goal at Con Ed: to ensure that a high percentage of qualified women is represented in the selection process.

Communication

Information on Con Ed's recruitment efforts is highlighted in internal publications. There has also been some video coverage regarding the number of women Con Ed brings into nontraditional fields. Additional highlights on the issue are communicated through a weekly e-mail bulletin.

Impact

Collaboration with existing nonprofit organizations has proved to be a successful recruiting strategy for Con Ed. Because of the success of Con Ed's partnership with the Blue Collar Prep Program, other companies have implemented similar recruiting efforts. These training organizations now have a much wider selection from which to choose. This has, in turn, created a more competitive atmosphere for recruitment, essentially providing women with greater opportunities and more options for their careers.

About fifteen to twenty women are hired per cycle (usually three or four cycles per year). In the last five years, women held an average of 22 percent of nontraditional jobs at Con Ed. This number is notable, considering the significant drop in overall employment at the company. The percentage of women in nontraditional jobs for the years 1993 to 1997 has been, respectively, 21 percent, 24 percent, 17 percent, 25.6 percent, and 21.2 percent.

Key Elements

- A high level of support and understanding of the program from upper-level management

- Pairing women with mentors

- Identifying critical staffing needs for training and recruiting

- Focus on getting women into operations positions, critical to advancement at Con Ed

HEWLETT-PACKARD COMPANY

Computers and precision instruments

Headquarters: Palo Alto, California

Employees: 121,900

Annual revenues: $42.9 billion (1997)

Catalyst Award: 1992 (Technical Women's Conference)

College Recruitment Practices

Historically, Hewlett-Packard has filled half of its external exempt positions through college recruitment. As one of the premier high-technology companies in the United States, HP recruits from a pool of the most talented young scientists, engineers, and business majors. To increase the size of the pool, make itself a highly attractive employer in a competitive recruiting environment, and diversify its workforce, HP sponsors what it calls a SEED (Student Education and Employment Development) program to funnel students into internships and, in many cases, into employment.

Of 975 college graduates hired by the company in 1996–97, 209 came through the internship program. In addition, the company hired 915 SEEDs. Given the high likelihood that these positions translate into future employment, HP focuses intently on recruiting women and traditionally underrepresented minorities. Nearly half of the SEED participants are women and nearly a third are members of underrepresented minority groups.

Teams of HP recruiters—volunteers who hold line positions at the organization—carry out the program's activities. HP targets eighty-four colleges and universities and interviews more than ten thousand students annually. To broaden their reach to women and minorities, HP attends seven annual conferences run by associations like the Society of Women Engineers, the Society of Hispanic Professional Engineers, and several others.

HP has established relationships with universities and primary and secondary schools throughout the country. The goal is to continue building and filling out the feeder pool. One example is the Diversity in Education Initiative, a multiyear, multimillion-dollar commitment with several universities and partnering K–12 school districts that attempts to increase the number of women and underrepresented minority students graduating in engineering. Other types involve sponsored internship programs, such as one in conjunction with Cornell University that provides annual scholarships to African Americans attending Historical Black Engineering Colleges to obtain master's degrees in engineering.

To measure its success, HP evaluates its annual acceptance rate, with particular attention to women and minorities, and surveys student perceptions of HP as an employer of choice.

HP intends to move its recruitment on-line in 1998, thus increasing its access to "exceptional students we're not meeting."

Impact

In 1996–97, HP successfully recruited an incoming class that was 36 percent women and 18 percent underrepresented minorities.

Key Elements

- Targeting colleges and universities, associations, secondary schools

- Sponsorship of internships and scholarships

- Beginning on-line recruitment

Leadership Development

J.C. PENNEY COMPANY, INC.

Retailing

Headquarters: Plano, Texas

Employees: 250,000

Annual revenues: $23 billion

Catalyst Award: 1995

Career Pathing

JCPenney, the nation's fourth-largest retailer, has a predominately female customer base and a large percentage of women associates. The continuing change in demographics and the openings occurring through the headquarters move in 1989 gave JCPenney the opportunity, as a company executive said, "to balance our workforce." The company's top leadership initiated a plan to increase opportunities for women in the organization. The driving force of the initiative early on was the Women's Advisory Team, whose nineteen management women and men worked with senior management to identify issues and foster the development of women. The company's comprehensive support for women combines an internal program for women's advancement with external events and support.

JCPenney subsequently merged its women's and minority teams into a Diversity and Work-Life Issues Team to support the company initiative. The company created the position of Director of Diversity and Work-Life Programs in 1996, a position that reflects the increasing importance of work-life balance issues in the company's thinking regarding its diversity business strategy.

One of the most important pieces of the initiative has been the company's career pathing tool (implemented in the early 1990s), which clarifies job opportunities through a grid comparing jobs by level, skills required, and criteria for the position.

Early on a mentor program was developed to support newly hired associates and associates transferring into the Home Office from the regions and stores. The program coordinator matches associates with a volunteer mentor in a senior position. This program, which is mandatory for associates, makes sure that new associates have a coach to support their orientation into the Home Office environment. The company has subsequently enrolled some of its high-performing women in an external mentoring program implemented in Dallas. As part of the developmental process, this program matches senior women with senior executives (mentors) from other companies. JCPenney has been a sponsor (along with other companies) in this program.

The company has paid particular attention to expunging assumptions about what associates are or are not willing to do to advance their careers. At one time, for example, the relocation might not have been offered to women whose managers assumed they were unwilling to relocate, for a variety of possible reasons. JCPenney now requires discussions with associates regarding their willingness to relocate, effectively eliminating the possibility of assumptions made in error. As part of the appraisal process, associates note their ability to relocate.

Accountability

Through the appraisal processes, developmental plans are discussed and career plans are outlined for female associates targeted to advance in the coming years. Senior management meets annually with a review team comprising the three top company officers to discuss goals and career plans for high-potential performers.

Impact

The impact of the Women's Advisory Team and more recently the Diversity Team has been significant. Women now hold 41 percent of geographic district manager positions and 36 percent of regional business planning manager positions.

Key Elements

- Strong support from company leadership
- Integration into Penney's business strategy

MOTOROLA

Electronics, wireless communication

Headquarters: Schaumberg, Illinois

Employees: 142,000

Annual revenues: $27 billion

Catalyst Award: 1993

Succession Planning With Clout

Motivated by changing workforce demographics, Motorola broadened its long-standing succession planning practice in 1989 to incorporate diversity objectives by accelerating the advancement of women and people of color.

The Initiative

Motorola's succession planning process, the Organization and Management Development Review (OMDR), features ambitious corporate "Officer Parity Goals" requiring that by year-end 2000 the representation of women and minorities at every management level mirror the national representation of these groups in specific areas of import to the company. It is unique in that it embraces entry and middle levels of management as well as the upper levels, which are more commonly the focus of succession planning. OMDR identifies the women and people of color who have the talent to reach senior levels, and requires plans for their development, holding managers accountable for the necessary development and retention.

In addition to reporting the representation of women in their organizations, senior managers must prepare development plans for high-potential individuals. Managers also complete Vice Presidential Planning Forms for women and people of color who are identified as having the potential to become vice presidents within a specified time period. These forms provide a road map that includes plans and time lines for promotions and lateral moves.

An annual succession planning form, the replacement chart, identifies key positions and three people who could fill each one: line one is the immediate successor who could step in immediately; line two is the person who should succeed the incumbent if the company had three to five years to prepare for the transition; line three is the most qualified woman or minority candidate at that time, in addition to any woman or minority person already on lines one or two. Women and minorities must be included, even if it means hiring from outside.

Accountability

The CEO drives the initiative with strategic assistance from the Human Resources Department. Human Resources monitors and provides analyses of the company's progress toward its officer parity goals, as well as the representation of women and people of color in each of the key areas and in staff versus line positions. Motorola believes that top leadership commitment is essential to driving such a process. Senior management must be convinced that no company can sustain success without using the diversity of talent available to it.

Impact

The initiative has produced results: in 1989, Motorola had two women vice presidents; in 1997, there were forty, including seven women of color.

Key Elements

- Strong leadership and commitment from senior management

- Broad definition of succession planning to include the widest talent pool

- Careful strategic planning for individual career development

- Clearly defined targets and goals

- Manager accountability for success

KNIGHT-RIDDER INC.

News and information services

Headquarters: Miami

Employees: 22,000

Annual revenues: $2.8 billion

Catalyst Award: 1996

Mentoring

Knight-Ridder, the newspaper and information company, is competing in a fast-changing, volatile industry. Understanding that it does business in a diverse world in which economic power is increasingly wielded by women as well as men, the company recognizes that newspapers and other forms of media need to reflect the communities they cover, both to maintain a standard of excellence and to be prepared to recognize business and product opportunities that might arise. In light of women's growing economic influence, Knight-Ridder wanted particularly to strengthen its position with women readers.

In 1989, Knight-Ridder's diversity task force created a mandate to advance women. All business units were required to develop numeric targets based on regional populations and to design programs to advance women to senior positions.

Bench Strength Program

Knight-Ridder's "Bench Strength" program is a formal mentoring system targeted at high-level employees, who are identified by senior managers at newspapers as being within two to three years of taking on significantly broader leadership roles. More than 40 percent of the participants are women. Corporate officers take responsibility for a group of six to eight mentees. Officers serving as mentors have a number of responsibilities:

- To talk with each mentee's editor or publisher to get an assessment of his or her strengths, weaknesses, and career aspirations

- To have a similar in-depth talk with the individual

- To have the mentees and their editors devise a career development plan, looking forward two to three years and including a timetable, a cost projection, and a clearly understood outcome

- To review the plan and fine-tune it with the editor and the individual

- To support and assist in implementing the plan and make sure the timetable is met

Officers meet annually to discuss the individuals in the program. This creates a familiarity with these individuals for the time when job openings arise.

Accountability

Knight-Ridder holds vice presidents and supervisors accountable for results for the Bench Strength program and all other diversity initiatives. At the corporate officer and local company executive levels, bonuses are tied to performance on advancing diversity, including women. Performance reviews also contain requirements relating to diversity hiring and development. From 1990 to 1995, Knight-Ridder significantly moved the needle on women and minorities in the workforce and management representation through a five-year diversity plan. More and more, however, diversity goals and efforts are becoming integrated into everyday practices and plans. Today, each company's strategic plan specifies steps toward its clearly defined goals for advancing diversity, including women, at management and nonmanagement levels. The elements of the plan include

- Any specific recruiting and hiring

- A program for accelerating the training and experience of women and minorities, identifying individuals and projecting assignments and opportunities

- A specific program for enlarging the pool of qualified women and minorities for jobs

- Plans for aiding organizations in the community that promote opportunities for women and minorities

- Plans for conducting diversity training (including gender, sexual harassment, and work-life issues) in the workplace

- Steps to be taken to assure both the reality and perception of fairness to all employees

Impact

Women represent about 40.1 percent of Knight-Ridder's workforce and they are equally reflected among its executive ranks, at 39.6 percent, up 17 percent from 1991. A survey of the papers' readers showed a significant increase in female readership from 1991 to 1994.

Key Elements

- Sustained effort over time

- High-profile support by top leaders

- Accountability built into the incentive structure

- Close alignment with business strategy

COOPERS & LYBRAND LLP

Professional services

Headquarters: New York

Employees: 18,500

Annual revenues: $2.5 billion

C&L Mentoring Initiative

Coopers & Lybrand, which has also increased its emphasis on work-life balance issues so that it may recruit, develop, and retain more women, designed the Women Partners' Leadership Conference to identify and address issues affecting women at the firm. The third conference took place in 1997. All members of the firm's Management Committee attended to emphasize the importance of fostering women's advancement. The chairman agreed to respond within sixty days to conference concerns, outlining a list of specific actions on goals achievable within one year.

Initiative

The chairman, in response to the most recent Conference, has indicated that as part of the firm's efforts to create competitive advantage throughout managing a diverse workforce, one hundred of the firm's top partners will assume specific responsibility for the mentoring and career development of one hundred high-performing women and minority managers. Called the C&L Mentoring Initiative, its goal is to have partners guide the development of their less experienced protégés, and increase their skills, achievement, and understanding of the firm. However, the manager mentee is ultimately responsible for his or her own development.

The firm defines *mentor* by describing what one does: guide, coach, support, teach, help, advise, counsel, advocate, clarify, affirm, and sponsor, and also serve as a friend, role model, sounding board, and constructive critic. From a mentor, mentees learn the values of the firm, have access to a role model and adviser, and develop self-confidence. Mentors have interactions with managers different from themselves, learn through teaching, and give something back. The firm benefits as future leaders are identified and assisted in their development.

The matchmaking process occurs as follows:

- Each line of business or business unit receives a list of partners rated as "exemplary" in the HR section of the partner evaluation form. The partner serves as Director of Diversity, and the line of business or business unit identifies the mentors. In addition, the entire Management Committee and all Cluster Managing Partners automatically serve as mentors. The list of mentors is publicized.

- Managers with at least three years in grade who are women and people of color and rated in Category 1 are reviewed and selected by the line of business or business units along with the Director of Diversity.

- Lines of business or business units assign mentees to mentors in order to capitalize on existing relationships; mentors may select mentees from the listing of top managers. Factors to consider include geographic proximity, line of business, and existing relationships.

The mentee, with mentor input, develops a career plan addressing assignments, training, and special assignments. The two must have at least one contact per month—perhaps just a phone call, perhaps a lunch or a meeting—and they meet at least once per quarter to assess progress and develop the relationship. Meetings may be formal or informal (social). The mentor is responsible for making sure these occur and for developing the relationship. The mentor or the mentee may terminate the relationship after six months, but the firm expects the relationship to last at least three to four years. A follow-up questionnaire to evaluate the program goes to all participants.

Lines of business have the option of expanding mentoring efforts beyond the scope of this program as business needs dictate.

Accountability

The mentor is responsible for developing the relationship, but the manager mentee is ultimately responsible for his or her own development.

Success Measures

The program, new at the time of publication, has created several ways to measure success:

- Retention of strong performers

- Admission to partnership

- Successful exit from the firm, for example, happily taking a job with a client or potential client

- Assessment of mentees on quality of the relationship and effectiveness of the counseling

Key Elements

- Diversity declared a business imperative

- Participation of Management Committee

KRAFT FOODS, INC.

Food production and distribution

Headquarters: Northfield, Illinois

Employees: 14,000

Annual revenues: $29 billion

Leadership Development, Mentoring

To guarantee itself a pool of talented future leaders, in 1992 Kraft Foods implemented a leadership development program, which it calls the LeaderVIEW Process. Actually a hybrid of executive coaching and mentoring, LeaderVIEW targets developmental needs of high-potential senior managers, who are identified during the succession-planning process. The program has the support of senior management, which has committed both financial and human resources to the project.

The Initiative

Each participant identified through succession planning works with one coach, who is generally selected from among the senior Human Resources generalists and management development specialists at Kraft. Typically, the ratio of participants to coaches is 2:1.

The process involves five distinct phases. During the *contracting phase*, the coach meets with the participant and the participant's supervisors to describe the process. During the *data-gathering phase*, a 360-degree assessment is sent out to supervisors, peers, subordinates, internal or external customers, and anyone else who might provide critical feedback. Next, the coach conducts highly structured two-hour interviews with the participant and supervisors. Discussions focus on the participant's work history, significant life and work experiences, strengths and weaknesses, and career ambitions. The coach then compiles the information obtained through these interviews and forms, identifies the strengths and weaknesses of the participant, and presents findings; this phase is called the *feedback phase*.

The next phase is *development planning*: the participant drafts a plan targeted at developmental activities and assignments, such as participation on special task forces or relationships with role models or mentors.

The final *three-way phase* involves a meeting with the boss, coach, and participant to discuss the detailed development plan.

Communication

Information about the program is communicated mainly through the succession planning process, leadership development programs, and development planning guides.

Accountability

Line managers are evaluated on the success of each participant's three-year plan. The company uses statistics on participation, number of coaches trained, and number of plan completions a year in evaluating senior managers.

Impact

LeaderVIEW has been well-received, as evidenced by the number of interested participants. From its inception, approximately 265 participants have completed LeaderVIEW, 80 of whom are women. There were 60 active participants in the fall of 1997, including 20 women. In a survey to measure the impact on individual management styles, 85 percent of LeaderVIEW participants indicated significant changes in their own management style (for example, leadership skills) since going through the process.

Key Elements

Kraft advises other organizations implementing leadership development initiatives to be sure to focus on the following:

- Commit financial and human resources to the project.

- Have support of senior leadership.

- Stay focused on who is targeted and who will participate.

- Develop measures for evaluating effectiveness and impact on the organization.

FEDERAL EXPRESS

Mail, packaging, freight

Headquarters: Memphis, Tennessee

Employees: 137,000

Annual revenues: $11.5 billion

Leadership Evaluation and Awareness Program (LEAP)

In the late 1980s, Federal Express began to recognize some challenges in its selection of managers. Some did not understand their jobs, and some who had done well in other positions had skills that were not well matched with the demands of their current jobs. The company began to see high attrition rates—up to 10 percent of managers either were terminated or stepped down. To reduce the undesirably high turnover rate among new managers, in 1989 Federal Express implemented the Leadership Evaluation and Awareness Program (LEAP).

The initiative had the support of top management, having been started by the chairman and then championed by the chief operating officer. A group of officers headed by an executive vice president began the process; the senior vice president of personnel was accountable for designing, developing, and implementing the process of LEAP. The company successfully piloted the initiative in an operating region.

The Initiative

Participation in LEAP is mandatory for all employees interested in becoming managers. The process is designed to evaluate a candidate's leadership potential and to force candidates to examine their own interest in and aptitude for management. It seeks to identify candidates who have the following nine leadership dimensions: charisma, individualized consideration, intellectual stimulation, courage, dependability, flexibility, integrity, judgment, and respect for others. These dimensions are specifically selected by Federal Express and were selected based on a study of successful managers.

A LEAP manual describes the four-step LEAP process. Future management candidates may nominate themselves if they meet the minimum criteria of education, experience, and employment in good standing. First, participants take an introductory one-day course entitled "Is Management For Me?" which familiarizes them with managerial responsibilities. They may opt out of the process at this stage.

Second, participants receive evaluations and coaching to improve leadership attributes. Over this three-to-six-month period, participants create an Employee Leadership Profile (ELP) that records specific experiences demonstrating their capabilities in each of the nine leadership dimensions. Managers then work with candidates on developing activities to strengthen any weak areas. FedEx stresses that the mentee must drive this learning process. Again at this stage, the participant may opt out.

At the conclusion of this process, managers make a written manager's focused recommendation supporting or opposing the participants' bid for management. Third, peer assessments are completed by coworkers selected by the candidate's manager. Colleagues of the LEAP participant complete confidential assessment forms indicating individual prospects for management.

Participants conclude their involvement in LEAP by appearing before a panel of three managers, diverse by gender and race and trained to serve in the LEAP assessment. This panel evaluates participants on their oral presentation skills and written responses to questions, with a focus on specific leadership scenarios. A subsequent interview determines receipt of an endorsement for leadership potential. Before issuing its opinion, however, the panel compares its findings with the Peer Assessment, Manager's Focused Recommendation, and the ELP. If not endorsed by the LEAP panel, candidates have at least six months to improve on deficient attributes and then have the opportunity to reapply. If endorsed, candidates become eligible for management positions.

Accountability

Human Resources maintains electronic records of all participants in order to track their performance and ensure candidates are performing at a level their endorsement says they should be. In addition, HR regularly tracks the LEAP process to monitor and ensure that proportionate numbers of women and people of color are being endorsed through LEAP. Upper management maintains constant endorsement and promotion of the program.

Communication

To avoid or overcome any resistance on the part of management, Federal Express has maintained an internal marketing campaign for LEAP, making use of internal publications, internal television broadcasts, posters, and presentations. The campaign emphasized the endorsement and involvement of the chairman and the chief operating officer.

LEAP, by allowing women to nominate themselves for management positions, eliminates potential bias of managers who do not want to promote women. When combined with job posting, it allows employees to push themselves into management. It also prepares candidates for a managerial position, as well as offering the option to opt out if they see management is not a good match for their skills. Another advantage of LEAP is that it provides managers with a pool of prescreened applicants, saving many steps in the hiring process; moreover, it encourages internal hiring, thus helping retain individuals with company-specific knowledge who may have tired of their current positions.

The company successfully piloted the initiative in an operations region.

Impact

In the first five years, approximately six thousand candidates completed the process, 76 percent of whom were endorsed by the LEAP panel; in 1997, 69 percent of managers at Federal Express were LEAP-endorsed. Impact studies show that female representation is larger than the percentage in the employee base and that women find the process to be fair and inclusive. By formalizing qualifications for management positions, LEAP has reduced subjective hiring decisions and given women and minorities greater access to management positions.

Management frequently revises the LEAP program to meet current demands of management. The company has added several training courses on coaching and managing leadership growth.

Key Elements

In adapting LEAP to another organization, Federal Express offers the following counsel:

- Determine leadership qualities particular to the organization.

- Ensure senior management support is constant and visible.

- Focus on design and development of training events to support the initiative.

- Track the results for fairness and goal achievement.

- Make the initiative inclusive.

- Encourage the mentee to drive the process.

THE KROGER COMPANY

Food and drug stores

Headquarters: Cincinnati, Ohio

Employees: 212,000

Annual revenues: $25.2 billion

Succession Planning in the Supermarket Industry

The largest supermarket chain in the United States, Kroger operates over thirteen hundred stores in twenty-four Midwest and Sun Belt states, plus approximately eight hundred convenience stores and thirty-five manufacturing plants. The Kroger Company established its number-one nonfinancial goal as increasing the operating management opportunities for women and minorities in the organization. Kroger values its diversity program because it fulfills the company's moral and legal obligation, extends access to the talents of all employees and potential employees, and provides broader perspectives to managerial issues.

The Initiative

Through careful analysis of the succession ladder, Kroger identified the store manager position as the key operating position for future promotions. Store managers receive training and operating experience that provide the skills needed for advancement to district manager, merchandiser, vice president, and on up. Since the goal of the company is to increase the opportunities for women and minorities, it was therefore incumbent on the company to maximize the opportunities for women as store managers.

Kroger corporate management approaches this goal systematically, first by initiating quarterly reviews of all store manager candidates in each division by gender and by race. If the number of women and minorities is small, management examines the reasons and develops a plan for improvement. Second, the company requests each division to project the number of store manager openings anticipated in the next year. Third, quarter by quarter, it reviews the list of individuals appointed to store manager positions that have opened during the quarter, then compares this list with the division's candidate list. If the number of women and minorities is small relative to the number of women on the candidate list, it seeks the reasons.

Accountability

Corporate management holds the division accountable.

Impact

The program represents the evolution of a documentation and accountability system that Kroger inaugurated in 1989. The system increased the number of women store managers by 49 percent in five years. The initiative has become an integral part of Kroger's succession planning process, which extends from corporate officers to the store manager positions. Development and career plans are written for new and current management; this becomes a key process in preparing candidates for top store and other management positions.

Key Elements

- Support from the top

- Identification of lynchpin job

- Systematic follow-through

- Monitoring of appointments

TEXAS INSTRUMENTS

Electronics

Headquarters: Dallas

Employees: 42,000

Annual revenues: $10 billion

Catalyst Award: 1996

Women's Initiative

The Women's Initiative began in 1989, when Texas Instruments chairman and CEO, the late Jerry Junkins, established five TI People Initiative Teams in response to changing demographics. After Texas Instruments sponsored an audit of its work culture, it established a diversity office in 1991. A work/life survey was conducted in 1992, and TI hired a work/life director. At the same time, several grassroots employee initiatives were under way. All of these efforts focus on developing programs to increase TI's business results and to respond to employee concerns, including pieces on career and personal development and work-life adjustments. Recently, TI has added a mentoring program and begun to sponsor a distinguished women's lecture series, bringing in four high-level women each year, and has held TECH 97, a conference sposored by women in technology. (For another look at TI, see the discussion of teaming up in the Benchmarking Culture section of Part II.)

TI created a worldwide diversity statement: "Our effectiveness at using the talents of people of different backgrounds, experiences and perspectives is key to our competitive advantage. Diversity is a core TI value. . . . We will create an environment where people are valued as individuals and team members and treated with respect, dignity and fairness." It continues, "Every TIer must work to create an environment that promotes diversity. An inclusive environment respects the individual and values the contributions of people of different backgrounds, experiences and perspectives."

Management demonstrates its commitment to the initiative by financial support and training opportunities. TI's grassroots organizations include the TI Diversity Network and women's, African American, Hispanic, Asian, gay/lesbian, and deaf groups.

Measuring Diversity

Not surprisingly, TI, as an engineering company, has developed several instruments to measure diversity and the progress of its initiative. The company uses these instruments to evaluate workplace, environmental, and cultural change and measure the progress TI is making toward an inclusive environment and culture. The measures include

- A partnership reporting system (that is, a survey to gather employee feedback on organization effectiveness)

- A culture audit

- A user feedback process (surveys or focus groups to assess employee opinions on specific initiatives)

- A work-life family survey

- A sexual harassment survey

Diversity objectives are measured in a format called *"Dashboard."* The Dashboard measures representation of women and people of color at various grade levels, pay equity, turnover (percent of running average), and number of new hires. A report is disseminated to management on a quarterly basis showing the status of measurement goals. Achievement of individual responsibility for growth, learning, and excellence is analyzed by:

- Training hours completed

- Individual development plans (one of TI's top 1997 priorities)

Communication

Each year, TI publicly reports its progress on women and minorities in three areas: hiring, promotions, and procurement from minority- and woman-owned companies. Within the company, business groups are also monitored on these commitments. Since Dashboard results are made public, this generates competition among managers to produce results. The results of the cultural audit, the partnership report, and other surveys used at the corporate level are available to employees and the specific findings can be used by TI Diversity Initiatives. This reporting of results raises expectations for action and TI's competitive culture forces managers to respond. In addition, when issues are identified, voluntary teams can form to address them.

Internal communication vehicles used by TI include the Values of TI handbook and the Worldwide Diversity Statement (referred to earlier); a quarterly newsletter that communicates activities and news from all TI's diversity initiatives, called *D NEWS*; site newspapers for employees; various diversity forums; flyers at TI sites, e-mail, and bulletin board displays; *T NEWS*, an on-line news service; an Internet home page; and various other TI publications and diversity brochures. Less formal communications on diversity continue through brown bag lunch forums, coffee talks with executives, and regular team meetings. In addition, TI publicizes diversity progress in major local newspapers through participation in two local covenants.

Accountability

While TI aims at individual responsibility and personal accountability, the company decided managers' year-end performance bonus would depend on "people values" including diversity as well as on financial and business priorities. Each business group is held responsible for developing and executing strategies and success measurements in diversity.

Key Elements

- Measures of progress

- Publicizing of results

- Managers' bonuses tied to results

Management Systems

NISSAN RESEARCH AND DEVELOPMENT (NISSAN MOTOR COMPANY)

Automobile manufacturing

Headquarters: Farmington Hills, Michigan (Nissan R&D)

Employees: 143,754 (Nissan Motor Company)

Annual revenues: $65.6 billion (Nissan Motor Company)

Integrated Human Resource System

Nissan Motor Company is a global corporation primarily engaged in the manufacture and sale of automobile products in Japan and overseas. Nissan R&D is the North American arm of the parent company, with nearly 80 percent of its workforce in engineering and technical positions. The Integrated Human Resource System is unique to Nissan R&D.

The Initiative

When Nissan R&D was centralized in Michigan in 1988, corporate leaders viewed the time as opportune for creating an integrated human resources system that would more effectively link corporate objectives with individual performance objectives. To facilitate the identification of individual performance objectives, the company spent two years producing an employee development tool, the Development Grids.

The Development Grids provide information about job competencies and performance levels for personal career growth. A team of line managers and human resource professionals developed the grids to:

- Organize jobs into one of seven job families

- Identify core competencies within jobs

- Establish formal behavior and performance measurements

By focusing on competencies, the company sought to enhance the flexibility and versatility of talent, as well as to improve mobility within job families, and to a lesser extent, into other functional areas. Each of the Nissan R&D job families—including engineering, technician, and professional—includes four or five progressive positions or career classifications. Competencies, a list of key skills, and measurements for assessing individual proficiency exist for each job. Consequently, the Development Grids function as career-pathing tools by outlining, on a career classification basis, performance criteria and associated levels of performance. Each individual staff member is therefore better able to understand performance expectations for advancement.

The Grids for each job family are arranged thematically and include such areas as job knowledge; organizing, planning, and prioritizing; and decision making. For example, one of the key competencies for organizing, planning, and prioritizing for an Engineer I is the "ability to make basic schedules," while an Engineer IV must have "ability to assess and forecast future needs and advance requirements." Another example of a competency is the "ability to solve major system problems." This competency is followed by a specific measurement: "Produces error free system solutions."

Once the Grids were complete, the Grid development team identified nontechnical competencies shared by all employees, such as leadership, program management, and communications. A Development Grid–based training program was then designed to support these competencies among all employees, regardless of job family.

Performance Appraisal Process

Nissan R&D's performance appraisal process is essentially the glue of the integrated HR system in that it aligns corporate and individual performance goals. The process begins with an assessment of the staff member's developmental needs. Next, by using the information outlined on the Development Grids, the staff members, along with their managers, create individual development plans consistent with their competency needs, corporate and departmental performance objectives, and individual, longer-term career interests. At the conclusion of the cycle, based on self- and manager assessment, employees are evaluated on their performance in the core competencies outlined in the Grids and the cycle begins again. Nissan R&D has instituted a strong incentive for participation in the performance appraisal process—failure to do so may result in staff members' being ineligible for inclusion in the annual salary review process.

The program has evolved since its inception in 1991. Developmental Grids are updated annually to ensure they capture important current engineering skills and requirements. In 1996, the entire training syllabus was revised to focus back on core skills.

Communication

Nissan R&D held training sessions to introduce the initiative. Since then it has sponsored numerous sessions devoted to explaining the initiative's objectives and process. Before its implementation, managers were trained in how to use the Grid program. The company continues to hold meetings and training sessions as necessary and communicates frequently by memo or newsletter.

Impact

The company is still in the process of defining competencies for its management positions. Nonetheless, it reports that because of the information the Grids provide, Nissan R&D staff now have greater understanding regarding job requirements and criteria for advancement within job families. One of the principal outcomes of this process is that individuals have become better informed, have assumed more individual responsibility, and have become active participants in their own career development. Equally important, staff members' interests are more clearly aligned with organizational and departmental objectives.

Key Elements

- Broad consensus and understanding regarding job competencies and requirements

- Linkage between the work of individuals and that of departments and the business

- Shared, formally stated performance criteria

- Effective performance appraisal process

3M

Manufacturing

Headquarters: St. Paul, Minnesota

Employees: 85,166

Annual revenues: $13.5 billion

Consensus Review Process

For decades, 3M has been a global leader in key markets, including industrial, consumer, office supply, health care, and more. The company began using the Consensus Review Process in 1989 as a pilot program in one of its manufacturing divisions. The process replaces the traditional one-on-one performance evaluation with group assessments of managers' performance. The purpose—and 3M's motivation for undertaking this process—is to gain a broader perspective on managers' skills and developmental needs.

It begins with directors holding meetings with their managers, executive directors with their directors, and divisional or staff vice presidents with executive directors and ending with group vice presidents meeting with their respective divisional vice presidents. Elements of each manager's or pre-manager's performance are discussed as documented against the previous year's developmental action plans. Employees submit an accomplishments résumé, which gives them an opportunity to highlight their key accomplishments.

Next the group reaches a consensus on each individual's evaluation and recommends actions for future development. *Actions* are defined as job moves, career-broadening assignments, skills development, and so on. Sponsors are listed for each action, which establishes who is accountable for assisting the individual with achieving the development goals. Gender and racial diversity are considered when actions such as job moves are being discussed, but are not specific goals of the process.

Accountability

Managers and pre-managers are required to participate in the Consensus Review Process, yet many divisions have also implemented it at lower levels. 3M's Human Resources department first developed the process in partnership with a manufacturing executive, and together they were the initial champions. Today, depending on the division, the process is driven by line managers with assistance from HR or by HR alone. The year-end meetings act as a type of accountability because at those meetings managers report the progress of their subordinates' developmental action plans. At 3M, managers are evaluated on how well they help their people develop.

Impact

As a result of the Consensus Review Process, 3M has more than doubled the actions taken on development plans. Managers and their subordinates have a clear focus on goals and action steps for the coming year. 3M has improved its data about the talent available and thus can create more diverse and accurate high potential lists. The process has had a positive impact on the culture at 3M, in that people are more receptive to development, coaching, and sponsorship. For employees, the process is also a plus because through the review meetings a broader range of managers learn of their skill sets and contributions, increasing their potential career opportunities within the organization. According to 3M, some twenty thousand people are now involved in the process.

Key Elements

- An explicit, documented development plan for the individual that includes actions for future development

- Employee documentation of accomplishments prior to the review

- Specific accountability for carrying out future development actions

- A group review process

- Managerial accountability for the development of subordinates

Work-Life Practices

■■■

EASTMAN KODAK COMPANY

Commercial and consumer photographic and digital products

Headquarters: Rochester, New York

Employees: 95,000

Annual revenues: $16 billion

Catalyst Award: 1990

Work and Family Programs

Kodak, the photo-products company, has had a decades-long commitment to work and family. Renewing that effort in 1986 despite budget cutbacks, Kodak took a leadership role in removing the barriers to women's advancement by appointing a task force to examine work and family issues. In 1996, the company underwent a corporate strategic effort that resulted in the combining of work-life and diversity programs. Kodak has widely publicized an expectation statement that by 2004, management ranks will reflect the markets that they serve.

CEO support is key to the success of Kodak's work-life programs. When George Fisher took Kodak's helm in 1993, he established what he called core company values and performance expectations that now permeate the Kodak culture; these values include

- Respect for the dignity of individuals

- Integrity

- Credibility

- Trust

- Continuous improvement and personal renewal

The CEO identified six business imperatives, which are widely communicated to all employees: employee development; health, safety, and environmental responsibility; building and managing a diverse workforce; strengthening the Kodak brand; customer satisfaction; and people leadership.

The Initiative

The task force began with a research phase that included benchmarking of thirty-three companies on compensation, benefit, and personnel practices; focus groups of employees and supervisors with each of the company's major facilities; consultation with work-family organizations; a "needs assessment survey" of two thousand employees; and a managerial review of recommendations that included managers from each business unit. In addition, focus groups were formed within each department to review the recommendations of the task force.

A year after the task force was formed, the chief executive and the corporate management council accepted its recommendations. Programs offered by Kodak include summer camp, employee networks such as the Working Parents League that target work-family issues, work-life seminars, a nationwide resource and referral service, flexible work arrangements used by thousands of employees, emergency backup care, family leave, adoption assistance, a dependent care expense program, and health and wellness programs.

Kodak was a founding member of the American Business Collaboration for Quality Dependent Care, described in the Work-Life Practices section of Part II.

Communication

Prior to implementation of each program, management and supervisory personnel learned of the programs through two integral systems, an electronic mail system (then cascaded to employees), and the *Management Newsletter*. At implementation, Kodak announced its programs to the general employee population through the house organ, *Kodakery*, which is frequently used to remind employees of available programs and to advise employees of how the programs are being used, including statistics. The company announced the nationwide resource and referral program and the adoption assistance program via a mailing to the home addresses of all employees. Kodak has produced a text for a Kodak Work and Family Program publication that has gone to all employees. Company representatives participate in local and national programs, symposiums, panels, and roundtable discussions to espouse work-life programs.

Accountability

Kodak has created a set of management performance commitment metrics (MPCM) to assess a range of performance criteria, 30 percent of which are directly tied to employee satisfaction. Individual members of the task force were responsible for writing the procedures and implementing the programs.

Impact

Kodak employees use the programs actively. From 1991 through 1996, 2200 took advantage of family leave, including 150 men. In 1996, 300 employees or family members used the child care resource and referral program. From 1994 to 1997, Kodak funding supported more than 900 child care and school-age programs.

Key Elements

- Support from top management, communicated by the CEO

- Senior management involvement

- Integration into the core values of the company

Kodak offers the following advice to other companies:

- Perform an up-front assessment of your needs.

- Work from the top.

- Use extensive communication.

- Educate managers and supervisors.

- Be inclusive; work-life is not just about women with kids, it's for all employees.

JOHNSON & JOHNSON

Pharmaceuticals and health products

Headquarters: New Brunswick, New Jersey

Employees: 82,300

Annual revenues: $18.8 billion

Balancing Work and Family Program

Johnson & Johnson is the world's largest and most comprehensive manufacturer of health care products serving the consumer, pharmaceutical, and professional markets. It is highly decentralized, with 168 separate companies worldwide. In 1989, Johnson & Johnson introduced its Balancing Work and Family Program.

The program with its various components was designed in large part to address the changing composition of the workforce: the increasing numbers of women, two-career families, single parents, and children of elderly parents. The comprehensive program includes the following components:

- *Child care resource and referral:* This service helps employees find, evaluate, and choose appropriate child care arrangements.

- *On-site child development centers:* There are four on-site centers.

- *Dependent care assistance plans:* Employees can use payroll deductions to transfer pretax earnings to dependent care accounts administered by the company.

- *Family care leave:* Job-guaranteed unpaid leave for up to twelve months may be used by male or female employees to care for a family member; this benefit serves as extended parental leave for employees with newborn or adopted children.

- *Family care absence:* Time off with pay is granted to provide short-term emergency care for family members.

- *Flexible work schedules:* The company encourages supervisors to respond to the needs of individual employees who experience changes in family responsibilities by developing flexible work arrangements, including flextime, part-time work, job sharing, and telecommuting.

- *Adoption benefits:* In addition to providing family care leave to adoptive parents, the company reimburses up to $3,000 for the cost of adoption and provides adoption referrals, adoption consultation, and support during and after the adoption process.

- *School Smart:* This resource and referral service assists parents in choosing public or private schools appropriate for their children, as well as answering parents' questions about their children's education.

- *Elder care resource and referral:* This service provides information on aging, expert help in choosing appropriate services, referrals to community services for the elderly, and useful publications.

- *Relocation planning:* Individualized relocation services, which may include reimbursement of moving expenses, are provided.

- *Employed spouse relocation services:* Assistance is given to a relocated employee's spouse in finding a job in the new locale.

Johnson & Johnson also provided work-family training for managers and supervisors to help them understand the business case for work-family policies and to help them implement effective work-family practices. The message stressed that family-friendly programs are aimed at helping the company attract and retain the top-quality employees needed to remain competitive in its industry. To underscore its commitment to family, the company in 1989 altered the fifty-year-old Company Credo for one of the few times in its history to include this additional responsibility: "We must be mindful of ways to help our employees fulfill their family responsibilities."

Communication

The programs are presented in brochures that are distributed throughout the company. The brochures also mention the study conducted in 1990 and 1992 that evaluated the impact of implementing the various programs (described in further detail later in this section).

Training

Johnson & Johnson provides work-family training for managers and supervisors. The training helps them understand the business case for work-family policies and helps them implement effective work-family practices.

Impact

Johnson & Johnson has evaluated the impact of its work-family programs through an employee survey administered shortly after the programs began in 1990 and again in 1992. The findings included the following statistics:

- Between 1990 and 1992, supervisors became significantly more supportive of employees when work-family problems arose.

- In 1992, 51 percent of employees "strongly agreed" that their supervisor was supportive when they had a routine family or personal matter to attend to, as opposed to 36 percent in 1990.

- In 1992, 40 percent of employees believed that their supervisors would *not* think that if one employee gets more flexibility, it will have to be given to all (up from 27 percent in 1990).

- Supervisors were also seen as more supportive of the use of flexible time and leave policies in 1992; 47 percent of employees (compared with only 37 percent in 1990) believed their supervisors understood that flexible work arrangements would not cause undue problems.

- Employee reports indicated that between 1990 and 1992 fewer work-related problems affected their personal lives.

Key Elements

- Commitment to work-family balance

- Availability of a wide range of family programs for employees

- Training for managers and supervisors to implement the programs effectively

- Evaluation process to assess the impact of the programs

MORRISON & FOERSTER LLP

Law firm
Headquarters: San Francisco
Employees: 1,565
Annual revenues: $220 million
Catalyst Award: 1993

Fostering the Advancement of Women in the Law

Morrison & Foerster is an international law firm headquartered in San Francisco, with offices in fourteen cities worldwide. Of the firm's 201 partners, 22 percent are women. In 1986, Morrison & Foerster was approached by United Way to help establish a consortium of Bay Area employers whose focus is the development of programs that support work-life balance. The firm became a founding member of what is now called "One Small Step," an association of nearly a hundred public and private employers, the purpose of which is to encourage, assist, and increase the number of Bay Area employers who assist their employees in balancing work and family responsibilities.

The Initiative

In 1987, the firm established a firmwide Work/Family Committee to develop programs on an office-by-office basis. The firm has set three goals in an effort to advance women:

- To create opportunities for women to obtain their highest professional potential, while enabling them to contribute to the communities in which they live and work

- To keep the work environment free of internal obstacles to women's advancement through ongoing training in gender and diversity awareness

- To remove the external barriers to women's ability to achieve their full potential through work and family programs

Morrison & Foerster has had in place—for over a decade—an array of work-family programs that help women in the legal profession achieve their fullest potential. These include a flextime policy for partners and associates with caregiving responsibilities, a three-month paid maternity leave (followed by a three-month unpaid leave), a family sick-leave and a firmwide dependent care resource and referral program; the firm views these as basic levels of support. Use of these programs by associates and partners shows that care of family members need not derail career advancement.

The firm will pay 95 percent of backup child care, either through in-home services or a local center. It also provides referrals for child and elder care, help with college selection, and loans and scholarships.

Diversity

Morrison & Foerster links its flexible work policies to diversity. It has established ongoing training programs to teach lawyers, managers, and staff how to work with one another in a diverse environment and how to manage in a workplace made more complex by the firm's commitment to flexible work arrangements for women. Lawyers are trained in preventing sexual harassment and delivering effective feedback; many of the programs are taught by partners who have received special training in these issues. By linking initiatives for female attorneys to its key business strategies, Morrison & Foerster ensures the endurance of its programs.

Communication

Programs are publicized monthly by posters, an internal Web site, and brochures, and quarterly in town hall meetings when the managing partners travel to each of the firm's offices to conduct meetings about firm activities, business, and policies.

Impact

It has been possible to recruit and retain valued employees while furthering opportunities for women. In mid-1997, 45 of 201 partners and 165 of 447 nonpartner lawyers were women. Female lawyers hold key positions at the firm, including chair of the Budget Committee, chair of the Attorney Personnel Committee, membership on the Points Committee (which determines partnership compensation), membership on the Policy Committee, and chair of the Morrison & Foerster Foundation. Women also serve as managing partners in several regional offices.

Key Element

- Targeting program to all employees on an entirely inclusive basis

---

DOW CHEMICAL COMPANY

Chemicals

Headquarters: Midland, Michigan

Employees: 62,000

Annual revenues: $20.2 billion

Catalyst Award: 1995

Relocation Assistance

The Dow Chemical Company is one of the country's twenty-five largest industrial companies, with more than half of its sales outside the United States. Diversity efforts date back to 1987 and include both national and foreign operations. In the late 1980s, the company recognized that the diversity of its workforce would be critical to its competitiveness and created a Diversity Steering Team of senior managers, as well as two advisory committees, to consider issues regarding women and minorities and recommend actions to Dow's operating board. Dow's "Blueprint for Diversity" included several innovative components, including relocation assistance for dual-career couples.

The Initiative

As part of Dow Chemical's diversity initiative, the organization recognized that many of its employees were in dual-career families, many of them dual-Dow families in which husband and wife are both Dow Chemical employees. In response to the increasing numbers of dual-career couples and the need for employees to relocate to advance, Dow decided to expand the dual-career assistance program to address the needs of the "trailing spouse."

When the company relocates a member of the dual-career family, it provides up to three months' reimbursement for a partner's lost income while he or she is looking for a job in the new location. However, if the couple decides to live apart, the company reimburses commuting expenses. To aid with the transition, the company offers extensive job-search assistance and career counseling available for partners.

In addition, Dow will refund the cost of tuition, professional exams, fees for licenses or certification, expenses for interview trips, and, for a cross-border move, assistance which can be in the form of reimbursement for services from an immigration firm to enable the partner to relocate.

Impact

Dow has found that the program has removed barriers associated with relocation of dual-career couples and made the relocation process a smoother one.

Key Elements

- Reimbursements for partners' relocation

- Job search assistance for partners

THE AMERICAN BUSINESS COLLABORATION
FOR QUALITY DEPENDENT CARE

The American Business Collaboration for Quality Dependent Care was formed in 1992 as a corporate response to labor force changes brought about by the increasing number of women and dual-income families in the labor force, the growing technological skill gap in new jobs, and the increasing caregiving responsibilities of employees. The collaboration is a strategy to increase the supply and quality of dependent care services around the country. By helping employees better meet their care needs, companies will attract and retain talented workers and help them come to work and be more productive. Collaboration allows companies to leverage their dollars, cover a wider geographic region, support a diverse variety of projects, and meet a greater range of employee and community needs.

Although programs made possible by the collaboration's sponsorship are for all employees, dependent care assistance is a key piece of any effort to promote the career development and advancement of women. The majority of working women give birth or adopt children during their careers and will have primary responsibility for child care arrangements as the children grow. Women also tend to be the primary caretakers of elderly parents.

Despite a great national need, there is no one caregiving model that will work everywhere for every family or individual. Within a population working at a company, employees have children and other dependents ranging from infants to children in school to elders. For each stage of life, dependent care needs differ. Parents with infants may seek in-home care; parents of school-age children may want them in more formal programs. Within the same population, caregiver preferences will vary with income, type of job, and cultural background. Shift or manufacturing employees, for example, are more likely to rely more on relatives for child care than are professionals who have relocated several times. So rather than promote a particular type of arrangement, several companies agreed to join together to tap and in some cases enhance or enlarge resources already available in communities and to encourage the development of new resources to serve employee needs.

These efforts are targeted at the needs of employees in the areas but also support existing community services. Community-based programs funded include day-care centers, family day-care training, adult day care, senior volunteer programs, and programs for school-age children. The collaboration also funds model programs that are national in scope and can be replicated in many diverse communities. The Boston-based consulting firm, Work/Family Directions, manages the collaboration.

During the first phase of the collaboration, from 1992 to 1994, 156 businesses and public or private sector organizations invested $27.4 million in 355 dependent care projects serving forty-five targeted communities. In the second phase, beginning September 1995, the chief executives of twenty-two champion companies signed a statement of support of the collaboration. The champions included such leading American companies as IBM, Hewlett-Packard, Xerox, and AT&T. The statement signaled a commitment of $100 million for the development of projects in more than sixty targeted communities over a six-year period, through the year 2000.

American Business Collaboration for
Quality Dependent Care: National Champions

Aetna	Citibank
Allstate Insurance Company	Deloitte & Touche LLP
American Express Company	Eastman Kodak Company
Amoco Corporation	Exxon Corporation
AT&T	GE Capital
Bank of America	Hewlett-Packard Company
Chevron Corporation	IBM Corporation

Johnson & Johnson   Price Waterhouse

Lucent Technologies   Texaco Inc.

Mobil Corporation   Texas Instruments

NYNEX   Xerox Corporation

Women's Workplace Networks

■■■

XEROX CORPORATION

Document processing systems and services

Headquarters: Stamford, Connecticut

Employees: 86,700

˙ Annual revenues: $17.4 billion

Employee Support Groups

Xerox Corporation is a document processing systems and service company with a long commitment to diversity issues. The company currently has many internal employee networks for various groups.

The Initiative

The first employee support group, or caucus, was formed in the late 1960s, as a result of national racial violence that alerted senior Xerox management to the reality of racial inequities. Initiated at a grassroots level, its original focus was primarily on African American employees in the sales force. Today there are four main caucuses, for African Americans, women, Hispanics, and gays and lesbians. The caucuses sponsor a range of programs and activities, including

- Workshops on a variety of topics such as interviewing skills, computer literacy, and presentation skills.

- Annual national and regional workshops on self-improvement and career development, culminating in a banquet featuring a Xerox senior manager and a keynote speaker from government or the business community.

- Informal mentoring for members of their constituencies.

- Outreach to new hires.

- Discussions about ways to improve management processes. These discussions have resulted in changes to the job posting program and career planning activities.

When employees first launched the caucuses, they faced several barriers that have now been overcome. It took some time to achieve recognition from Xerox and acceptance from other employees. There were also funding difficulties (the caucuses are employee-run and initially operated at their members' expense) and time constraints; Xerox allows the caucuses to meet in company facilities, but does not provide company time for the meetings. Therefore, they are held on weekends.

Although Xerox is not responsible for any implementation or accountability concerning the caucuses, the company does support them by providing distribution lists for them to use when recruiting, allowing them to use duplication facilities for mailings, and providing substantial funding. Now each caucus receives more than $30,000 per year toward a national conference, with the exception of the gay and lesbian group, which receives approximately $10,000 per year because it is relatively new and small in size.

Each caucus has a corporate champion who works with the group. This champion may attend meetings, provide additional support (either financially or operationally), or open doors for the caucus within Xerox. While the champion is not accountable for the success of the caucus, he or she is a channel through which the group contacts Xerox management.

Communication

To maintain communication between the two entities, the CEO created a related forum, known as the *Round Table* discussion. Organized by the Diversity Department, this annual meeting incorporates the caucuses into corporate efforts to address employee concerns. Participants present issues for discussion at the meeting. Concerns brought back from the meeting are then examined by the Diversity Department and changes are made in the necessary area.

Impact

The caucuses have had a significant impact on the company culture. They have provided a welcoming environment for minorities in the company, as well as helping it diversify recruiting efforts and sponsored scholarships. If problems arise with any minority employee, the caucus attempts to work toward a solution.

Development of the caucuses has been notable. The number of caucuses has grown, as has the size of each. With this growth, the caucuses have also increased their activities. While the focus of the caucus groups was initially on self-development, they have expanded to include community outreach programs. Community involvement, career counseling, and scholarship funds have been a few of the ways Xerox's caucuses have tried to offer opportunities to Xerox minority and female employees as well as the nation's workforce.

Key Elements

- Appointing a liaison to communicate between Xerox and the caucuses

- CEO involvement to ensure communication across groups

- Financial support and use of equipment and facilities from Xerox

BAUSCH & LOMB

Eye care products

Headquarters: Rochester, New York

Employees: 13,000 worldwide

Annual revenues: $2 billion

Women's Executive Network

Bausch & Lomb's Women's Executive Network (WEN) began as a strategic task force created by executive women, at the request of the chief executive, to assist the organization in addressing issues related to women's advancement and to support the company's diversity initiative. At first a highly mobilized task force, WEN first identified areas for strategic action on the part of the company, pointing to recruitment, career development, succession planning, networking, showcasing commitment and success, and executive involvement in cultural change. These areas later evolved into subcommittee activities. As a task force, WEN was responsible for implementing pilot programs; after their implementation, WEN members continued to audit the programs and to act as advisers.

Like many of today's women's workplace networks, the Women's Executive Network continues to serve as a resource to senior management. Working with the organization's diversity office, the minority network, HR, and other groups involved with the diversity initiative, the network has provided gender-focused resources and assistance in implementing the diversity strategies of those organizations.

In addition, it offers mutual support, communication, counseling, training, coaching, and information flow among its members by providing a supportive, success-enhancing environment focusing on the attraction and retention of women at all levels of the organization. It encourages the formation of other employee networks within the company. It has piloted mentoring programs, initiated a series of discussions with high-potential women about career options, and created opportunities for women in the organization to network. One of the organization's subcommittees has assisted in the formation of regional and divisional networks outside the corporate area.

One of the most original accomplishments of the Bausch & Lomb network was the creation of what it calls the "Executive Diversity Checklist." To help senior management better understand their role, the network created this tool to outline what actions individual executives could take to create a business environment that fosters women's advancement. The Executive Diversity Checklist was circulated to senior managers. The list follows:

Bausch & Lomb Executive Diversity Checklist

- When a developmental opportunity arises (an internal task force, an executive education course, a cross-functional rotation), I make sure that women are considered.

- I participate in a regular review process to ensure that women are progressing satisfactorily against established measures of progress.

- I personally serve as a mentor to at least one female manager, and each of my direct reports does the same.

- I host at least two business-related social events per year in which management women can participate comfortably.

- I support women employees' networks and meet regularly with their representatives to discuss gender-based issues in the company.

- I send clear and frequent messages to my team that fostering diversity in management is important to the productivity and competitiveness of the company and that I am personally committed to it.

- I actively intervene in meetings or conversations in which interrupting, stifling, or other behavior infringes on the full contribution of women participants.

- I respect the fact that the majority of my employees are part of dual-earner or single-parent families and make it possible for them to balance work and personal responsibilities by supporting use of policies such as flexible work and parental leave.

- I provide occasions for female directors of my company to meet with executive and management women.

- I serve as a director, volunteer, or member of at least one organization in which I am in the minority by gender or race.

- I have a system for identifying and developing high-potential managers and ensure fair representation of women in that pool.

- Women in my company are well represented in line management positions and in functions from which senior managers are typically drawn.

Key Elements

- Resource to senior management on gender issues

- Piloting mentor programs

- Assistance to other networks

BANKERS TRUST

Financial services

Headquarters: New York City

Employees: 15,228

Annual revenues: $9.6 billion

Initiatives for Women

In the 1970s and 1980s, Bankers Trust underwent an organizational transition and turned itself from a commercial bank into an investment bank. In part the bank's goal was, in the words of one bank official, to create a "pure meritocracy," a decentralized, intensely entrepreneurial culture with virtually no bureaucracy to impede the creativity of its employees. After a successful transition, in the early 1990s the bank reorganized its human resource services. The reorganization consisted of three separate but overlapping initiatives designed for the Bankers Trust culture.

The Initiatives

"Globalization and Diversity" had the goal of building a global, integrated culture by attracting and developing diverse, high-quality talent. Efforts focused on non-U.S. nationals, U.S. minorities, and women. *"Global Employer of Choice"* involved adopting programs that help employees balance their work and family commitments. The bank surveyed the firm to establish a measurement baseline for retaining women, developed a formal family-work policy and guidebook, and instituted a backup child care program.

Simultaneously, a grassroots effort among women managers led to the *Global Partnership Network for Women*, which was created in 1991 to help career development, leadership, and business opportunities for women. Because Bankers Trust is decentralized, the network provides its members with a broad overview of the firm's business areas. It strives to further career development, leadership, and business opportunities for women by providing networking forums, seminars, and business events. The network fills critical business needs by bringing together panel discussions on client strategy, presentations to employees by the chairman, and a networking forum that provides an overview of all the firm's business lines.

The GPNW calls its leadership structure "fluid and democratic," with little bureaucracy or layering. Women fill leadership positions as work permits; there are no voting positions, no elected positions, and no dues. The steering committee meets every four to six weeks, attended by thirty to forty women. Bankers Trust's Globalization and Diversity budget funds GPNW activities, workshops, and programs, except for the annual conference, which is directly supported by business heads whose backing is solicited by women members.

The 1997 conference and workshops had a budget of over $200,000. Each January, the group meets to evaluate the past year's focus and establish the new year's objectives. It identifies a particular issue each year and builds programs around that issue. Some of these include networking, business development, communication, career development, and leadership development.

The network holds breakfast meetings with senior- and junior-level women as a way to network and share information. These meetings help women connect with each other and help generate business deals. Initially, the breakfasts were women-only events, but they have now been opened to men as well—and are as successful as ever.

The GPNW helps facilitate internal mobility and career advancement; networking has helped several women move laterally and vertically throughout the firm. The network has also helped increase the number of female MBAs who accept offers from Bankers Trust.

Communication

The network developed a Web site that includes articles from over fifty publications, a discussion forum for women on Wall Street, links to on-line services, and commentary from senior women on

Wall Street, who share keys to success and answer questions in a bulletin board forum. GPNW uses videoconferencing to establish connections among its members. It has held more than seventy events since 1991, in New York, London, Nashville, Los Angeles, Sydney, and other cities around the world.

Impact

GPNW began with a small group of senior women in 1991 and has grown to approximately 750 members, the majority in New York and Europe, although there are members in Hong Kong, Singapore, Tokyo, and Australia.

- The number of new female managing directors has increased from about twenty-five to over a hundred.

- Many women are now mentoring other women at the company.

- There is an increase in high-potential prospects and successor candidates for management positions who are women.

- GPNW facilitated the roll-out and use of the internal job posting system for professionals, which has increased internal mobility.

- GPNW has established a major external presence on Wall Street through an annual "Women on Wall Street" conference, in its fourth year in 1998.

- The 1997 conference was attended by over sixteen hundred professionals, forty of whom were Bankers Trust clients; the rest were a mixture of Bankers Trust employees and other Wall Street professionals. Highlights of the event included a panel of high-level women discussing leadership, along with three small-scale workshops attended by three hundred women.

Key Elements

Bankers Trust offers the following advice for other companies:

- Know your organization and be flexible.

- Solicit help from other organizations.

- Adopt a mentee organization and share experiences and knowledge.

- Leverage internal resources.

DAIN BOSWORTH INCORPORATED

Brokerage firm and investment bank

Headquarters: Minneapolis, Minnesota

Employees: 1,900

Annual revenues: $400 million

Association of Women Brokers

Dain Bosworth is a full-service investment services and investment banking firm with sixty-seven offices in eighteen states, mostly in the Upper Midwest, Rocky Mountains, and Pacific Northwest. The program sponsored by Dain Bosworth for women brokers grew out of grassroots efforts by women at the firm. The Association was founded in late 1991 to address barriers to advancement for women at the firm. Women in sales felt isolated in large territories in a field dominated by men, and many women felt a need for training and mentoring in how to win clients' trust and gather assets.

The Program

The Association of Women Brokers has been a catalyst for women brokers at Dain Bosworth—advancing their professionalism and success, creating a more supportive environment, increasing their retention rates, and making the firm more attractive to recruits. Not only has the association met its own objectives, it has paid handsome dividends in unexpected areas such as the identification of women with management potential, the naming of the first woman branch manager, and the creation of other women broker groups.

The Association of Women Brokers is a management-supported, member-driven organization. The association lists the following reasons for its existence:

- Encourage and mentor women brokers in a male-dominated field.

- Enhance members' professional expertise.

- Increase members' annual sales.

- Help Dain Bosworth recruit and retain women brokers.

All the firm's female brokers and many trainees are members of the association. Women are admitted after their second year at the firm, one year before they graduate from broker-trainee to broker.

The centerpiece of the association is its annual conference. The firm's female brokers vote on the program topics, serve on a program development committee, and organize their own two-day event, which is heavily subsidized by the firm. The annual conference strengthens relationships between women, affords opportunities to swap sales ideas, and provides a tool to become more successful at Dain Bosworth.

The group's production enhancement committee runs three successful programs: the "quantum leap" group, whose members commit to a significant increase in their annual sales; the "dialing for dollars" group, which holds a monthly conference call on sales-related topics; and the "mentoring" group, which coordinates formal mentoring relationships and holds a luncheon for women in each new broker trainee class.

The association reports to the firm's president and CEO, which entails an annual performance report and monthly conference calls with the CEO. The firm's top officers and other senior women executives usually attend the annual conference.

Communications

The group's communications committee prepares an annual directory, a member newsletter, and recruitment materials. It also facilitates an informal phone network to support members in times of need that range from failing to meet sales targets to being diagnosed with breast cancer.

Dain Bosworth staff learn about the association from quarterly newsletters and from articles circulated when the association makes news. New female brokers learn about the association during the recruitment process, and association members call to welcome them when they join the firm.

Accountability

The association is self-directed. The president of the board is responsible to the membership and to the three committees, and the membership gives advice and feedback to the board. Every year, the president of the association gives a presentation on the association's activities to Dain Bosworth's executive committee. That report includes details on the production of its members compared to that of the firm's male brokers.

Impact

Women brokers have gained greater recognition at Dain Bosworth since the association was started. The firm is now actively recruiting women as interns and experienced brokers.

During the first three years the Association of Women Brokers existed, the number of women brokers rose to eighty-nine from forty-four. Women were 12 percent of the sales force at the end of June 1997, up from 6 percent at the end of 1991. The association has also boosted members' sales production—even faster than that of the male brokers—to the point that they've nearly matched the male brokers' average performance. For example, in 1996, members' production rose 22 percent to $283,000, compared to an increase of 15 percent to $299,000 for the firm as a whole. (Women brokers who did not attend the last two conferences saw an increase of only 14 percent that year.)

Key Element

- Balance between grassroots support and support from the top

MCDONALD'S CORPORATION

Food services

Headquarters: Oak Brook, Illinois

Employees: 174,000

Annual revenues: $9.8 billion

Catalyst Award: 1994

Women Operators' Network for Franchise Owners

McDonald's Corporation's "Partnership with Women" encourages and recognizes the contributions that women bring to all facets of the business. The company's formal mission statement declares that "McDonald's USA will be viewed as the recognized leader for women in franchising and as the company of choice for women entrepreneurs." McDonald's commitment to developing and enhancing long-term business relationships with women is particularly exemplified by its unique partnership with its Women Operators' Network (WON), which is composed of women franchise holders. The company believes its workforce and its franchise owner-operators should reflect the diversity of the communities in which McDonald's does business.

WON, which began formally in 1988, shares the values of the corporation and is dedicated to the expansion of entrepreneurial opportunities for women throughout the McDonald's franchise system. WON has the full support of the chairman and senior management. The group's management liaison reports directly to the top officers of the company and provides the group with a communication link to management.

A key element of the network is the Spouse Certification Program, which offers spouses of existing owner-operators the training necessary to gain their own legal owner-operator status. WON's leadership works with regional managers to identify women who are eligible for spouse certification. WON members also serve as mentors who provide extensive support to program participants and all McDonald's employee networks.

Impact

Through the partnership, McDonald's has realized a 300 percent increase in female franchise owners. And today, McDonald's has the highest number of female- and minority-owned franchises in the fast-food restaurant industry.

The Women Operators' Network is an important part of McDonald's total quality management philosophy. By providing a forum for the exchange of information and ideas on such topics as running a profitable business, improving customer satisfaction, enhancing community relations, and resolving problems, senior executives credit WON as their most successful example of their total quality management program.

WON also serves as a model for other networks within McDonald's. For example, WON works closely with the McDonald's corporate women's group, the Women's Leadership Network.

Key Elements

- Network for otherwise separated franchisees

- Support from chairman and senior management

- Feedback to and from corporate management

- Option for spouses to receive franchise training

- Member mentorship of other McDonald's employees

Gender Awareness Training and Safety Training

■■■

CORNING, INC.

Manufacturing, building materials, glass

Headquarters: Corning, New York

Employees: 20,000

Annual revenues: $3.7 billion

Zero-Tolerance Sexual Harassment Policy and Training

Corning is a manufacturer of optical fiber cable and photonic components, high-performance glass for television and other electronic displays, and other advanced products for scientific and environmental markets. In 1986, Corning introduced its "Zero Tolerance" approach to eliminating sexual harassment. The program was created in response to the rulings in the landmark case of *Meritor v. Vinson*, which established that a hostile or offensive work environment is unlawful under Title VII. Corning had two principal objectives: to prohibit and efficiently deal with sexual harassment, and to ensure that sexual harassment does not undermine the company's "Total Quality" initiative to "unleash the potential of every [employee] and develop teamwork within every workgroup, and across units."

The Program

Corning's position on sexual harassment is simple. Sexual harassment will not be tolerated in any form. The company asserts that "sexual harassment is counterproductive to Corning's commitment to a quality work environment that is free from all forms of discrimination." Corning's policy includes a definitive explanation of sexual harassment and details the proper channels through which a complaint is reported. It also briefly explains the procedures that follow a complaint.

Corning encourages supervisors and team leaders to take a positive role to ensure that the work environment is free of sexual harassment and to work with Human Resources representatives to determine how best to initiate an investigation. Sexual harassment complaints are always investigated.

First, the employee is encouraged to speak with the individual who is allegedly committing the offensive behavior. If the problem persists, the employee can go to the person with whom she or he feels most comfortable—the supervisor or team leader, a representative of Human Resources/Employee Relations, a representative of Counseling & Support Services, or any member of the management team. Corning believes that offering employees these options helps ease an already difficult situation. Human Resources becomes involved as soon as the complaint is registered, regardless of who receives the report. A thorough investigation is completed. Both parties, as well as any witnesses, are interviewed internally in a confidential and objective manner. If the allegations are substantiated, then the individual who committed sexual harassment is dealt with according to the severity of the action. Penalties can include demotion, transfer, or time without pay.

If the allegations are found to be false, no action is taken against the person who initiated the inquiry as long as there is no indication that malice was involved. Corning policy states clearly that the company will not tolerate any "retaliation against the individual who raised the complaint unless it is found that the complaint was intentionally false." Follow-up counseling for both parties is recommended and can be arranged by contacting an HR/Employee Relations representative or the Counseling and Support Services within Corning.

Communication

Corning presented the policy in a brochure distributed company-wide. The policy defined

- Sexual harassment

- Corning's position on sexual harassment

- The role of the supervisor

- What is involved in an investigation

- Effects of substantiated and unsubstantiated allegations

- Steps that a supervisor or employee should take if sexual harassment is suspected

A variety of other methods are also used to communicate Corning's commitment to the elimination of sexual harassment. First, Corning includes a statement about its sexual harassment policy in the *Code of Conduct* manual. Second, members of Corning's Legal Department speak to employees on a regular basis. Third, the policy is distributed to all Human Resources and Personnel departments. It is also posted throughout the company in common areas where it will be visible to all employees, such as the coffee and copier rooms. A copy of the policy is available for anyone upon request.

Training

Corning has adopted training as another means to preventing and eliminating sexual harassment. The training is administered during orientation as part of diversity training. Supervisors and managers are trained to ensure that the work environment is free from sexual harassment. Ad hoc training is provided in accordance with complaints as well.

Accountability

Senior management supports the initiative through the Compliance Council, which is responsible for putting forth the *Code of Conduct*, an employee handbook for Corning. The council is composed of approximately seven members of the Legal Department and high-level staff from across the organization, including one senior vice president, two vice presidents, the head of Security, and several Human Resources managers.

Impact

The number of discrimination cases in litigation has declined for a number of years at Corning. Although there are no specific measures that can tie these results to the sexual harassment policy or training, Corning feels this decrease is a clear reflection of the substantial effort the company puts forth to address the issue.

Key Elements

- A strong, clear statement that sexual harassment is not acceptable

- A reporting process that allows employees access to a number of people for initiating a complaint

- The use of a variety of communication channels for disseminating the policy

- Continual reenforcement of the policy

- Continual training about the issue

- Termination among possible penalties

- Senior management commitment to the policy

UNITED TECHNOLOGIES CORPORATION

Aerospace

Headquarters: Hartford, Connecticut

Employees: 173,000

Annual revenues: $2.3 billion

Harassment-Free Workplace

United Technologies Corporation (UTC), the giant aerospace corporation, had compliance in mind when it added sexual harassment prevention to a diversity initiative already in place. But an even more powerful motivator—the bottom line—was present. UTC takes a three-pronged approach to compliance and diversity management challenges: cost, customer, and commitment. The goal is to avoid the cost of litigation, in time and money; to avoid any action that would tarnish the company's reputation with the customer; and to encourage employees to give their fullest to UTC. Employees will not stay where they are harassed, UTC's leadership believes.

The Initiative

UTC offers training in sexual harassment prevention, in a program that includes lectures and case studies as well as extensive interaction between the participants and the trainers. Any employee can take the course; all supervisors are required to take it. More than ten thousand of UTC's Connecticut-based employees have gone through the training.

The company also sponsors a poster campaign in its domestic and foreign operations, putting all employees on notice about the policy, the definition of sexual harassment, and the procedures for reporting harassment.

Communication

One of the biggest challenges for a company of UTC's size, domestically and globally, is communication. Few members of its large hourly workforce have access to computers, so the company cannot disseminate information solely on-line. In addition to its poster campaign, UTC communicates with employees about the harassment policy and training programs in the company magazine and via annual messages to the heads of each operation.

Accountability

The Director of Workforce Diversity reports directly to the presidents of the various units of UTC, to the chief executive's office, and to a committee of the board of directors. Every year the president of every company signs an affirmation of the policy, agreeing to enforce it. Discipline is generally the responsibility of a supervisor.

Impact

The company monitors the number of complaints filed against it with the state commissions on human rights or equal opportunity, to make certain there are no dramatic changes in the number of actions. The number of complaints has not risen in recent years.

Key Elements

- Match between initiative and overall company philosophy

- Wide understanding that harassment involves many potential costs to the company, economic as well as legal

UTC offers the following advice on diversity to other companies:

- Mean what you say. Enforce your own policies.

- Build relationships with universities and secondary schools through a range of activities, including educational programs, research, and scholarships.

- Support the development of an interest in science and technology early on. Target children and high school students.

- Emphasize recruitment of an integrated feeder pool through internship programs.

- Improve connections and visibility at minority and women's professional associations and networks, including the Society of Women Engineers (SWE) and the Society of Hispanic Professional Engineers (SHIPE).

DUPONT

Chemicals and petroleum

Headquarters: Wilmington, Delaware

Employees: 97,000

Annual revenues: $43.8 billion

Personal Safety Program

In the early 1980s, DuPont, the largest chemical producer in the United States and one of the leading chemical producers in the world, recognized the need to address personal safety issues and began by publishing personal safety travel guidelines for its female employees. The company also called in outside consultants to conduct rape prevention training. Response to the training indicated that more was needed. DuPont conducted a needs analysis and identified three key factors for a successful program:

- Manager support

- Companywide recognition of rape as a social issue, not a "woman's issue"

- Concern for all employees' personal safety needs

The Program

DuPont developed its Personal Safety Program to help employees address such social issues as sexual harassment, physical assault, spouse battering, child and elder abuse, and confronting rape in a responsible and meaningful way.

The program was initiated by the company's personnel development section of Human Resources (now the Diversity Education Development Group within Human Resources). This committee endorsed the program and has regularly reviewed its progress as it has spread throughout the company. The program began full operation in January 1986, and continues to be available companywide. It is linked to the larger objective of concern for the safety and respectful treatment of all employees.

Rape Prevention Workshops for female employees are included in the program and are available during working hours and on weekends. Wives and adult female dependents of employees are also welcome to attend. These eight-hour workshops are voluntary. The workshops address options and strategies to help prevent rape, as well as ways to cope with the aftermath of rape. They also address the company's procedures, guidelines, and resources for dealing sensitively with victims of rape.

DuPont recognized the need to provide training for managers. Half-day workshops for managers and supervisors were established. These video-based workshops help define managers' roles in helping employees who have been raped on or off the job, describe immediate needs of rape victims, address corporate guidelines for rape victims, and stress the concern for confidentiality.

DuPont also offers a Facilitator's Training Program. DuPont employees volunteer to be trained in this program. These volunteers implement the Personal Safety Program at the local level, and they identify local victim resources.

Other components of the program include

- Corporate guidelines ensuring confidentiality for rape victims

- A confidential rape crisis hotline available to all employees

- Legal assistance providing information concerning matters such as criminal and civil prosecution

- Assistance in handling external publicity that might result from a trial

- Full disability benefits (up to six months' leave with pay) and coverage of much of the cost of medical and psychological treatment through company health plans. This includes payment of all costs if the assault occurred in the course of business.

Senior management agreed to update the corporate policy on treatment of employees who have been assaulted or raped. Management agreed to invest the time and funds necessary to develop a first-rate training program. Many strategic business unit leaders have attended the Managers' Workshop.

DuPont has begun to offer other training programs related to personal safety and diversity awareness, such as understanding sexual orientation and male-female communication. The rape prevention program continues to be considered essential for raising awareness about the issue. The core curriculum of the training program includes the following workshops:

- *Women and Men Working as Colleagues*, designed to enhance participants' awareness and effectiveness in dealing with coworkers of the opposite sex

- *Efficacy for Professionals of Color*, designed for the employee of color who wishes to take personal responsibility for enhancing his or her professional development

- *The Men's Forum*, designed to address men's exclusion in a man's world

- *Sexual Orientation in the Workplace*, an effort to enlighten employees on issues relative to sexual orientation

- *A Right to Dignity: Understanding Battering*, which focuses on understanding the many facets of battering in relationships

- *Multicultural Awareness Workshop*, a five-day residential program that helps the organization explore the dimensions of diversity as they relate to the business environment

Communication

Listings of available workshops, along with descriptions, are communicated to employees through line management, in internal publications, at meetings, through an electronic bulletin board, and during developmental sessions.

Impact

The majority of DuPont employees have participated in the programs. One direct outcome of the initiative includes the development of *A Matter of Respect*. This is a workshop that focuses on establishing a responsible and respectful environment free of sexual harassment and discrimination. The *Rape Prevention Workshop* has developed into a highly recognized and valued program among women in the company. Women are not the only ones who gain from this workshop. There is an increased awareness and sensitivity regarding issues of rape and sexual harassment among men in the company as well.

DuPont believes that these programs provide many secondary benefits, including contributing to a supportive work environment and to improved productivity, addressing previously ignored areas of mental stress among employees, and opening communication lines between men and women.

DuPont employees know that there is zero tolerance for sexual harassment and abusive behavior of any type, be it due to race, sexual orientation, age, or any other factor. This awareness has been fully integrated into DuPont's company culture.

Key Elements

- A strong, clear statement that harassment is not acceptable

- Voluntary participation in all programs, some of which are open to family members

- Training for managers

- A wide variety of communication vehicles to promote the initiative

Epilogue:
Summing Up and Looking Forward

Companies now have more than one generation of women in their professional and managerial ranks: women who entered corporations and professional firms in the late sixties and early seventies—sometimes referred to as the pioneers—and women who have come in recently. There is a considerable age gap between these women, but more important, one finds a basic difference in the expectations they bring to business organizations.

The earlier generation of women, as reported in Catalyst's *Women in Corporate Leadership: Progress and Prospects*, found they had to work harder than men and that they encountered significant obstacles in their careers. There were few of them to support each other. There were few, if any, programs to help them balance work and family responsibilities, and where such programs existed, few women felt it safe to use them. Companies at that time did not experience turnover of women as a significant bottom-line loss because there were fewer women.

Statistics show that among the earliest group of women, those who made it to senior management made different choices from the average American woman. Fewer of them married; more of them divorced; and a larger percentage of them either chose not to have children or had fewer children than the norm.

Over the past two decades, substantial positive changes in the culture and work environment have occurred at organizations where these women worked. Many companies now have a critical mass of female professionals and managers, and pipelines bulging with talented women. The cost of turnover of female talent has become a compelling business case for many professional firms and a number of companies, especially service organizations. Work-family programs have become mainstream, though women on the fast track still hesitate to use them to their full extent.

The companies and firms whose best practices are found in this book are a decided minority in American business: a minority that includes many of the largest, most successful, best-run companies and firms in the country, but a minority nonetheless. Diversity is still off the radar screen of many organizations. In Catalyst's experience helping organizations develop some of the best practices found in this book, companies and firms willing to embark on an effort to create a woman-friendly work environment share at least these qualities:

- A top layer of leadership willing to commit long-term resources to the endeavor. "The critical issue is to make a long-term commitment," says Paul Allaire, chief executive of Xerox. "You have to build a base to have an environment friendly to women."

- A vision of the possibilities inherent in the synergy between the initiative and the strategic direction of the organization.

- A clear understanding of the business imperatives implied by the demographic changes expected in the workplaces and marketplaces of the immediate future and their relationship to the organization's goals. "We are very much a women's company," says James Preston, chief executive at Avon, "about 99 percent of our customer base and our workforce."

- Leaders willing to learn from the people around them and open to genuine change. Paul Allaire finds a "refreshing honesty" in the fast-track younger women at his company who won't sit still—or stay late—to obey the more pointless rules of the corporate game, like face time.

- Leaders with working daughters, like J. Michael Cook, chief executive at Deloitte & Touche, and H. Laurance Fuller, CEO of Amoco, who have firsthand experience to relate, or leaders, like James Preston, who had a female mentor.

- A belief in equality, even when the main impetus of an initiative is the bottom line. Joseph Pichler, chief executive at Kroger, the supermarket chain, credits the religious education he received as a young man for motivating him to start a diversity initiative. To John Bryan, chief executive at Sara Lee, a commitment to equality in the workplace was no different from the commitment he had made years ago by joining the civil rights movement in his home state of Mississippi.

- An awareness of the value of linking a company's business goals to wider issues, thereby leveraging the company's reputation and resources. The Avon Foundation, the philanthropic arm of the beauty products company, now focuses its money and energy on women's health and education, including outreach programs and early detection of breast cancer.

But the leading-edge companies see the sort of evolutionary progress that business tends to feel comfortable with and trust. "We're now thirty years into the women's movement," says James Preston. "A lot of women went into the professions. Now they have two

H. Laurance Fuller, Chairman and CEO, Amoco Corporation

When the phrase "gender diversity" gets thrown about in conversations among interested executives, the male-dominated oil patch doesn't typically arise as an example of a leading-edge industry. Yet one of diversity's more visible proponents is the chief executive of Amoco, the largest American oil company. Lawrence Fuller helped institute programs to diversify the workforce at the company and accelerate the upward mobility of women and minorities. He makes it sound like an issue that some would say is still controversial is settled in his mind. "No one of importance would argue that there shouldn't be a diverse workforce," he says flatly.

That is in part because he benchmarks Amoco against business in general, not against other technologically oriented—and female-challenged—petroleum companies. By looking where women are more numerous, it was hard to avoid the conclusion that to have access to the most talented people, Amoco would have to intensify its efforts to retain and promote women.

decades of experience. I think we're going to see a surge of women into board seats and managing partner positions."

Companies will need to be able to respond to these demands because they have no choice. Gender diversity is here to stay in the workplace. Jerry Choate, chief executive at Allstate Insurance Companies, counsels his corporate peers to continue to look to flexible work arrangements as the area most likely to need fine-tuning. "Balancing work and business life is becoming more and more complicated," he says. Family arrangements keep changing; companies

It did, in part by tying 20 percent of executive bonuses to meeting retention and advancement goals. With some exceptions made for working in certain hostile regions of the world or at jobs that require a lot of physical strength, "at Amoco we basically have women doing everything that men do," Fuller says.

Amoco pushed diversity by pitching its programs to men and to women. And it forcefully articulated the business reason for recruiting a diverse workforce. No one, Fuller contends, wants to hear the company is embracing affirmative action or diversity to "do the right thing." Women and minorities fear tokenism, white men fear what they see as inequity. Business people need business reasons to motivate them.

Fuller says if there is personal motivation in his support for diversity, he says it was seeing his three grown children, two daughters and a son, earn degrees from distinguished universities and take up careers in business. One daughter left a firm because it was not as "women-friendly" as it should have been, he says. But the careers of all three made him realize the wide spectrum of talent available to companies. "It brought home to me the fact that there is a lot of talent out there that should be given a chance," he says.

cannot operate as if the traditional arrangements are in place and still expect to get the best talent. "We have to respond," he says.

By taking Eastman Kodak aggressively into foreign markets, CEO George Fisher is at what most people would consider the next leading edge: internationalism. Fisher points out that diversity means not just race and gender, but other cultures as well. Cross-cultural diversity in a globalizing workforce is clearly one of the diversity challenges. Motorola is meeting this challenge by recruiting Japanese women into its offices in Japan, finding that it can recruit some of the top talent because these women have not been in demand by Japanese companies.

The new generation of women in U.S. business organizations takes the changes in the workplace for granted. They bring expectations to the workplace that are different from those of their older female colleagues. They are impatient. They expect flexibility and opportunity. They expect a level playing field. They are vocal about their expectations and their disappointment when companies fail to meet them. These women have raised the bar on what companies will have to do to attract and retain female talent. They will present new challenges to companies to implement flexibility. Since most of them will be part of dual-career relationships, their spouses and significant others will also be putting increased demands on their companies to organize work and measure productivity in different ways.

Some company, somewhere, is at this very moment creating new approaches to these new challenges that other companies can learn from. Catalyst will continue to benchmark and learn from these best practices and to assist other companies in meeting the challenges of gender diversity.

Part III

Resources: The Catalyst Award

For eleven years we have presented the Catalyst Award to corporations and professional firms for outstanding initiatives for women's advancement. Each of the initiatives described here has emerged as a winner after the highly selective evaluation process conducted every year by Catalyst. Each provides solid evidence of what can be done to effect change for women. Each is unique, yet each is replicable. With each new initiative to advance women, America comes closer to dismantling the barriers to women's upward mobility in corporations and professional firms. As go these barriers, so go barriers to maximizing our nation's economic strength.

We present the Catalyst Award–winning initiatives together here both to honor them and to inspire others, adding the application guidelines so that potential candidates for the award can see the mark they're aiming at. We look forward to the informed dialogue this presentation will provoke.

Sheila W. Wellington
President, Catalyst

The Catalyst Award Winners
1987–1997

Catalyst Award Winners:
Year by Year

Catalyst Award Winners: Programs

1987: Statewide Initiative

Connecticut Consortium for Child Care

Catalyst honored the Connecticut Consortium for Child Care for its creative solution to child care issues. Four Hartford-based companies formed the consortium in 1982 to respond to employees' unmet child care needs. A public-private partnership, it eventually expanded to encompass the entire state of Connecticut. The mission remained constant—to create an innovative child care referral service to help working parents become more knowledgeable about selecting children's day care and to enhance the ability of working parents to combine parenting and employment.

Corporate involvement was strong. Public and voluntary sector participants included the Connecticut Department of Human Resources, the Connecticut State Department of Human Resources, and the Private Industry Council. The consortium contracted with the Capital Region Education Council to coordinate such services for corporations as seminars for employees and training for in-house counselors. United Way's INFO-LINE provided a statewide information and referral service. The consortium successfully mobilized the public, private, and voluntary sectors to create a comprehensive and statewide child care plan. Participating companies could expect enhanced retention of valuable employees after parental leaves.

1987: The Equitable Financial Companies

Collaboration of Women's Business Resource Group

At the Equitable Financial Companies, President and CEO John B. Carter and the Women's Business Resource Group of senior female employees worked together to identify and address the career and work-related needs of the companies' female employees. The group looked at the companies' annual employee survey to help identify those needs. The survey provided a foundation of facts and information on which to base policy recommendations, and the group solicited further information directly from employees as needed.

Issues addressed included the adequacy of complaint mechanisms, salary and career progress, and the management of work and family roles. Carter took responsibility for implementing the plans discussed, and his senior staff kept the group informed of the progress of the plans. The Women's Business Resource Group and management evolved an effective partnership that addressed the concerns of both employees and management in a changing corporate environment.

1987: IBM

National Child Care Referral Service

To meet the needs of its workforce—with its increasing number of two-career and single-parent families—in 1984, IBM instituted its Child Care Referral Service. A national program that went beyond referrals, it initiated programs to increase the supply of child care providers nationwide and to enhance the quality of the care provided.

The results of the IBM referral service served as testimony to the extraordinary emphasis the company placed on its employees' welfare. The program increased the productivity of employed parents who knew their children would be cared for during the day; at the same time, it enhanced recruitment for the company. The service also educated parents, informed them about quality child care options, and through funding stimulated the growth of the number of child care providers and other resources in various communities.

1987: Mobil Corporation

Senior Management Development Program
for Women and Minorities

By creating the Senior Management Development Program for Women and Minorities, Mobil Corporation moved aggressively to identify and challenge high-potential employees and ensure that they had the opportunities and exposure necessary to advance to full potential. Mobil created the program when it realized that the programs it had in place were not resulting in some of the company's best people reaching the levels that the company had projected.

Mobil started the program in 1986 with several expectations. The company expected to create a larger, stronger group of female executives and executives of color at the highest levels. It expected to challenge and make full use of all internal talent. And it expected to create recognition in the employment marketplace that Mobil was committed to maximizing the career potential of all its employees. A high level of involvement from all executives, from the board's executive committee to each manager down the line, ensured accountability for the program. The program used profiles of the career paths of successful white males as models, and a careful screening process enabled participants to move to line positions.

1988: Avon Products, Inc.

Communication System for Managing Workplace Diversity

Avon Products realized the strong link between managing diversity in the workplace and the company's success and profitability. In March 1988, women represented 70 percent of management, and three women served on the board of directors. Avon, with its multicultural workforce, had innovative training, development, and education programs, as well as networks for people of color to discuss career-related issues.

The network groups communicated the issues to a multicultural committee, which reviewed them and made recommendations for change. One such change was the introduction of a study that tracked the upward mobility of women and people of color. Another was the Corporate Women and Minorities Committee, founded by CEO Hicks Waldron, which met monthly to check the company's progress in meeting its objectives to promote upward mobility and to ensure access to management for women and minorities. Not only did Avon provide its employees with a forum for the discussion of workplace issues, it also provided educational programs to give managers a better understanding of how to tap the potential and productivity of a diverse workforce—something Avon understood as a key to its competitive edge in the industry.

1988: Corning Glass Works

Quality Improvement Process Promoting Women's Advancement

The process of assessing women's advancement at Corning Glass Works grew out of the Total Quality Program, designed to promote quality throughout the company. In April 1987, CEO James R. Houghton recognized that the success of the program depended on tapping and developing Corning's female workforce.

One result of this mandate was the Quality Improvement Team—a task force designed to upgrade efforts in the recruitment, retention, and upward mobility of women in management. The team had support from top management and input from both line and staff managers. It recommended career development strategies to improve the upward mobility of women, as well as new recruitment efforts, the implementation of a diversity education program, communication of policies and practices regarding women, the development of community initiatives to encourage women to work at Corning, and child care and part-time work initiatives. Corning's concept of "total quality" fed into an integrated plan to promote women's career and leadership development.

1988: E. I. du Pont de Nemours and Company

Personal Safety Program

Through its comprehensive Personal Safety Program, DuPont addressed in a business context social issues such as sexual harassment, physical assault, spouse battering, child and elder abuse, and particularly rape. Senior management recognized that employees' concerns about safety both on and off the job could prevent them from fully reaching their potential. DuPont's program contributed to a supportive work environment and improved productivity by helping employees address previously ignored areas of physical danger and mental stress and by opening the lines of communication between men and women.

The program included companywide safety meetings, rape prevention workshops, workshops for managers to help define their role in working with employees who are survivors of rape, and corporate guidelines and services, including full disability benefits, to support the employee in the aftermath of rape. After participating in the program, a number of employees indicated that they had averted potentially dangerous situations due to their increased awareness. DuPont pioneered this safety program to help women and men cope with the issue of personal safety and thus enhance their productivity.

1988: Gannett Company, Inc.

Partners in Progress

The Partners in Progress program, instituted in 1979 by Gannett Chairman Allen Neuharth, encompassed strategies for recruiting, hiring, developing, and promoting women and people of color. The initiative included such goals as establishing diversity as a management objective and moving women into management positions.

Gannett started to track results in 1981. When Gannett received the Catalyst Award, 17 percent of its top executive vice presidents and general managers were women, as were four of the seventeen members of the board of directors. Close to 25 percent of Gannett's newspaper publishers were women as well, and the company's employment of women in professional positions had increased to 41 percent.

Partners in Progress helped establish Gannett as a leader in its industry by promoting the process of developing talent in a broad spectrum of people.

1989: Fannie Mae

Business Strategy for Women's Upward Mobility

Fannie Mae had focused on both recruitment and retention of women. CEO David O. Maxwell worked aggressively with top management to promote the company's most promising women. Together, they designed career paths and succession-planning schemes for individual women and sponsored the participation of these women in business programs at educational institutions. Fannie Mae held senior managers accountable for promoting women into management positions; human resources representatives monitored progress throughout the year and reported to the president, the CEO, and senior executives.

Maxwell said of their initiatives, "The day we're working toward is the day management is blindfolded, like Justice, to all forms of discrimination; to the day when women are recognized as leaders without regard to their gender."

At Fannie Mae in 1981, 4 percent of senior managers were women; in 1988, the number reached 26 percent.

1989: IBM

Elder Care Referral Service

Catalyst recognized IBM for outstanding work to help employees balance work and family responsibilities and in turn to help the company meet its business objectives. IBM was prompted to do this by data suggesting not only that persons aged sixty-five and over are the fastest-growing population group, but also that women would be the employee group most affected by elder care responsibilities.

On February 1, 1988, IBM introduced its Elder Care Referral Service, the first corporate nationwide consultation and referral service available to U.S. employees, retirees, and their spouses who need help for themselves or for older relatives. IBM collaborated with the consulting firm Work/Family Directions to develop the service.

The service offered personalized telephone consultation, consumer education, and referrals through a nationwide network of two hundred community-based organizations. Chairman of the Board John F. Akers said, "The IBM Elder Care Referral Service was established to help employees with the often complex and sometimes stressful responsibility of caring for aging relatives. In turn, IBM benefits because of higher employee morale, commitment, and productivity."

1989: U S WEST, Inc.

Women of Color Project

In 1989, U S WEST Chairman and CEO Jack A. MacAllister said, "Our effort to achieve a pluralistic workforce—that is, one in which the skills, talents, and abilities of a diverse employee body are recognized—isn't just idealism. It makes good business sense." Because of this commitment to pluralism, in 1988 U S WEST implemented a plan that identified non-Caucasian women to fill leadership positions. The program grew out of research conducted by employee resource groups. The findings included the insight that career impediments may be greater for those not in the racial or ethnic majority. The program did not guarantee promotions; it afforded these women the opportunity to compete for them.

The first fifty women of color were selected from a pool of eighteen hundred applicants on the basis of their leadership, communication, and decision-making skills. They received individual leadership training, a detailed five-year career plan, and a one-week survival course. Nearly half the participants in the program were subsequently promoted. Senior management companywide showed its support by volunteering as mentors to the women in the program.

1990: Eastman Kodak Company

Work and Family Programs

In 1986, management at Eastman Kodak Company recognized that in order to be competitive, the company must be known as a superior place for women to work. So, despite budget cutbacks, Kodak took a leadership role in removing the barriers to women's advancement by appointing a task force to examine work and family issues.

The task force reviewed the compensation, benefits, and personnel practices of companies supportive of work and family issues, consulted with top organizations in the field, and surveyed two thousand of its employees aged twenty-one to fifty. In addition, focus groups were formed within each department to review the recommendations of the task force.

A year after the task force was formed, the CEO and the corporate management council accepted its recommendations. Highlights of the resulting policies included a nationwide child care resource and referral service, family leave, adoption assistance, flexible work arrangements, and a dependent care expense program.

Kodak's employees used the programs actively. From January 1988 through March 1990, 649 employees, including 37 males, took advantage of up to seventeen weeks of unpaid, job-protected family leave. In the first fourteen months of the child care referral program, 1600 employees or family members used the service. During the same period, Kodak funding supported nearly 570 new family day care homes that provided spaces for more than three thousand children.

1990: John Hancock Financial Services

Innovative Family Care Initiatives

The John Hancock Financial Services commitment to child care began with the conviction that when employees win, the company wins. The company strategy was to recruit and retain top talent in

Boston's tight labor market. Recognizing the business payoffs of helping employees balance work and family, a corporate task force spent
two years in the late 1980s researching, designing, and implementing
a wide range of benefits and several unusually innovative programs.

In October 1988, John Hancock introduced an elder care assistance program and a flexible spending account that allowed employees to pay dependent care costs with pretax dollars. The
company then created two policies without precedent: a travel policy enhancement, in which employees for whom travel was an exception to their job description were reimbursed for dependent care
expenses incurred through business travel, and a policy that gave
employees who were parents access to a telephone to check on children arriving home from school.

In October 1989, John Hancock CEO E. James Morton announced a family care mission statement, along with new programs:
training for managers on work and family issues, three paid absence
days for family care annually, an expanded flextime program, a one-
year leave of absence with subsidized benefits, activities for employees' children during school holidays, reimbursement of up to
$2000 for adoption expenses, a trade fair of summer camp informa-
tion, and the building of an on-site child care center. Morton said
of the programs, "We believe every successful business must provide
tools, including child and elder care policies and benefits, that help
employees to balance their career and family goals. Such tools will
assure that 'Mommy' and 'Daughter' tracks will not derail the careers of some of our most valuable next-generation leaders."

1990: US Sprint Communications Company

An Integrated Approach to Managing Career and Family

In its short history, US Sprint Communications Company had experienced negligible attrition due to family-related concerns. But
demographic shifts prompted the company's farsighted management
to anticipate future retention and recruitment problems, especially

for qualified women. Thus, in keeping with the company's business strategy to attract and retain the best and the brightest, US Sprint created and implemented its FamilyCare program—and did it in just five months.

FamilyCare provided flexible work schedules, a dependent care resource and referral service, adoption assistance, personal and family counseling, working-partner relocation assistance, and flexible health care benefits. The company communicated the program extensively among its employees, and the program met and even exceeded its goals. As a result of FamilyCare, the company experienced increased productivity and the flexibility needed to attract and retain its quality workforce.

1991: Arthur Andersen and Company, S.C.

Access to Achievement

Arthur Andersen was the first professional services firm to win the Catalyst Award. The winning initiative consisted of two parts: a flexible work program and awareness training in workplace gender issues.

At Arthur Andersen, managers who at some point had worked part-time were eligible for partnership. Both female and male employees could return to work on a part-time basis for up to three years following the birth or adoption of a child, and they would maintain full-time benefits.

The company's workplace gender issues awareness training focused on enhancing interpersonal communication between male and female employees. In 1991, women represented over 40 percent of Andersen's over four thousand annual campus hires.

1991: SC Johnson Wax

Valuing Individual Potential

From the time the company's founder articulated his belief in the importance of his employees in the 1920s, SC Johnson Wax has worked steadily to create programs designed to attract and retain the best and the brightest of the workforce. Its programs have provided extensive training and development, assuring that women can acquire the skills to qualify for management positions. The company encouraged management to consider qualified women for new openings and reviewed pay and benefits structures to ensure those openings were equitable and attractive to women. The company also boasted an effective job-posting system. As a result of the programs, women were represented throughout the company's operations and businesses. SC Johnson Wax sought to promote from within whenever possible, and therefore, ongoing training and development were critical to the company's success. Starting in the 1960s, the company paid full tuition for employees' undergraduate and graduate studies.

1991: Tenneco, Inc.

Integrated Leadership Initiatives

As a company involved primarily in manufacturing, natural gas pipelines, and shipbuilding—nontraditional fields for women—Tenneco faced major challenges when it turned its attention to helping women advance. It rose to the challenge with an integrated approach that both encouraged the recruitment and promotion of women and provided a support system to help women achieve their potential.

Tenneco established the Women's Advisory Council in 1988 to identify concerns and create solutions. The council was responsible for the company's Work/Family Support Program and a 1990 conference of female managers. Their executive incentive program based a significant portion of each division's executive bonus pool on whether that division met all its stated goals and objectives for hiring and promoting women and people of color. The company found that success depends on an environment where both female and male employees can thrive.

1992: American Airlines

Innovative Career Management

American Airlines earned an award for its multifaceted approach to retaining, developing, and promoting women. The company's succession-planning process, known as Supertrack, required officers to submit detailed, cross-functional development plans for all high-potential women in middle management and above. Through the Career Development Program, an extensive job-posting program, employees could signal interest in a position even before the vacancy occurred. Through a related program, called Walk-A-Mile, employees interested in learning about the day-to-day responsibilities of a position could shadow the person in that job for a time. In addition, a task force was formed that worked to identify barriers, to educate female employees on the growing opportunities for women in technical fields, and to provide mentors for women in the company.

This comprehensive approach paid off: the percentage of women in mid- and upper-level management rose from 12 percent in 1986 to 21 percent in 1991. In the same period, women's representation at all levels of management rose from 30 percent to 39 percent.

1992: Continental Insurance

Advanced Development Program

Continental Insurance's Advanced Development Program identified high-potential employees and helped them attain key leadership positions in the company. The goal of the program was to cultivate talent from within, with the intention of moving more women into visible leadership roles; therefore, management ensured that many of the program's participants were women.

Once a year, Continental selected candidates through a rigorous process that resulted in a class of six to ten participants. The program's participants trained intensively for three months and formulated detailed career plans that included three to five assignments, with at least one geographic relocation. Experiences included staff, line, home office, field, project, and management positions, each twelve to twenty-four months in duration. Continental assigned an adviser, a manager, and a supervisor for coaching and feedback to each participant.

Senior management strongly endorsed the program, and this endorsement helped its success. Women, who represented over half of Continental's professional workforce, were represented equally in the process.

1992: Hewlett-Packard Company

Technical Women's Conference

A successful grassroots effort by company women resulted in Hewlett-Packard's first Technical Women's Conference in October 1988. The conference showcased female engineers and scientists in the company. In 1991, a worldwide Technical Women's Conference drew eight hundred attendees, twice the number of the first conference.

The 1991 conference included addresses by the CEO and by female senior managers. Female engineers and scientists presented their work in a series of technical sessions, and the conference provided numerous career development workshops. The company presented awards to recognize and enhance the visibility of female engineers and first-level managers. Management strongly supported the conference: they held it in a year when they canceled other corporate conferences, and they contributed their time in many ways. Management considered the conference consistent with Hewlett-Packard's tradition of fostering and supporting innovative activity and expected it to result in improved recruitment and retention of experienced technical women.

1993: Consolidated Edison

Commitment to Women With Technical Talent

While Con Ed had long sought talented employees regardless of gender or ethnicity, attracting women to a company where most jobs require physical labor had been a challenge. Motivated by changing workforce demographics and a bottom-line concern to develop and diversify management talent, Con Ed created a comprehensive strategy called Commitment to Women With Technical Talent to recruit, develop, and promote qualified women. The highlight of this strategy was the Management Intern Program, which Con Ed launched in 1981 to intensify the recruitment of women and to develop the future managers of the company. While women made up only 17 percent of engineering students nationally, they were more than 30 percent of the employees in the Management Intern Program. The program recruited approximately thirty college graduates annually on the basis of technical competence, leadership potential, and communication skills.

Con Ed also acted as a cosponsor of the Blue Collar Prep program, which aimed to prepare women educationally, psychologically, and physically for nontraditional jobs. In addition, the company provided work and family programs, a job-posting system, mandatory diversity and sexual harassment awareness training for managers, and informal networks for women at all levels of the company.

Besides cultivating future company leaders, the program improved retention: 75 percent of the eighty-nine female engineers hired since 1981 still worked at Con Ed at the time the initiative received the Catalyst Award. Through Commitment to Women With Technical Talent, Con Ed created a model for training and developing women who begin their careers in areas generally dominated by men.

1993: Morrison & Foerster

Fostering the Advancement of Women in Law

Morrison & Foerster, an international law firm with over six hundred attorneys in fourteen cities, was the first law firm to receive the Catalyst Award. Of the firm's 230 partners, 20 percent were women. The firm based its initiative on three strategies:

- Create opportunities for women to reach the highest professional level they are capable of while enabling them to contribute to the communities in which they live and work.

- Keep the work environment free of internal obstacles to women's advancement through ongoing training in gender and diversity awareness.

- Remove the external barriers to women's ability to reach the highest level they are capable of.

The company had pursued these goals by creating an array of liberal work and family programs, in place for over a decade by the time of the Catalyst Award. The firm also provided ongoing training for attorneys, managers, and staff on how to work together in a diverse environment. In addition, attorneys and firm managers received training in preventing sexual harassment.

Morrison & Foerster's efforts succeeded. The chairman made a continuing effort to place female attorneys in positions of power and prestige within the firm, such as the chairmanships of important committees. The firm management provided strong support of pro bono work related to women's issues. By linking strategies for female attorneys to its key business strategies, Morrison & Foerster ensured the endurance of its program.

1993: Motorola

Succession Planning With Clout

In 1986, Motorola initiated a systematic plan to accelerate women's advancement. Succession Planning With Clout featured the ambitious, companywide Parity Initiative, which required that by the end of 1996, the representation of women and people of color at every management level would correspond to those qualified in these groups in the general population. In September 1989, Motorola had two female vice presidents. By the time it received the Catalyst Award, the number had reached fourteen.

Motorola used its Organization and Management Development Review (OMDR), a succession-planning process that held managers at every level accountable for developing and retaining women and people of color. Each year, business unit managers distributed the OMDR package through the ranks, and division heads developed lists of high-potential individuals and submitted them to upper management. Career plans were devised for these high-potential women, men, and people of color, and managers were held accountable; when a woman or person of color left the company, her or his manager was responsible for ascertaining and reporting the reason.

In addition, in 1991 and 1992 the company conducted a well-received series of Women's Leadership Conferences to showcase the talent of Motorola women.

1994: Bank of Montreal

Workplace Equality Initiatives

In sheer numbers, women dominate the banking industry—except in the senior management and executive ranks, where they have represented a clear minority. Bank of Montreal found this unacceptable. Its initiatives to promote women were the first initiatives of a company based outside the United States to win the Catalyst Award.

In January 1991, the president and chief operating officer sponsored the Task Force on the Advancement of Women. The task force's groundbreaking report, culled from information in the bank's human resources database, proved that in terms of education, length of service, dedication, and job performance, women in the bank equaled or surpassed their male colleagues. The task force also identified the main barriers to women's advancement and set out action plans to remove them.

The task force called for the creation of a new department, Workplace Equality, responsible for implementing its recommendations and for ensuring a fully integrated approach to cultural change within the bank. The Workplace Equality team oversaw various initiatives, including gender awareness workshops, flexible work arrangements, child care, elder care, the revision of policies to support and reflect diversity and equality perspectives, a national career information network, and an executive adviser program. In addition, the team monitored the annual business plan process, in which all managers set goals for hiring, retaining, and advancing women and people of color, and the quarterly performance review process, which ensured accountability. The team approached tracking through a variety of channels, including employee feedback compiled in a report to the chief operating officer.

The results were impressive—between October 1991 and October 1994, the proportion of women promoted into the executive ranks increased from 29 percent to 50 percent; promotions into senior management increased from 20 percent to 38 percent; and promotions into middle management increased from 43 percent to 67 percent.

1994: McDonald's Corporation

McDonald's Partnership With Women

The initiative of McDonald's for the advancement of its female employees took the form of a partnership between the corporation and its Women Operators' Network, dedicated to the expansion of entrepreneurial opportunities for women throughout the McDonald's franchise system. Together, they worked to ensure that the company's workforce and franchise owners and operators reflected the diversity of the communities in which McDonald's does business. The network began operation with the full support and involvement of Chairman Michael R. Quinlan and of senior management, and its management liaison reported directly to the top officers of the company.

One key element of the network, the Spouse Certification Program, offered spouses of owner-operators the training necessary to gain their own legal owner-operator status. In another element, network members served as mentors for employees in all of McDonald's employee networks.

From 1989 to 1994, McDonald's realized a 300 percent increase in female franchise owners, and their stores produced some of the top-level financial rewards in the system. At the time of the award, McDonald's could boast the highest number of franchises owned by women and people of color in the fast-food industry.

The Women Operators' Network became an integral part of McDonald's. Its role within the company expanded to include recognizing and rewarding talented women employees, providing a forum for the exchange of information and ideas, and serving as a model for other networks within the company.

1994: Pitney Bowes, Inc.

Strategic Diversity Plan

In August 1992, Pitney Bowes, led by Chairman and President George Harvey, formed a task force to create a strategy to solidify the company's long-standing commitment to valuing a diverse workforce. The twenty-four-member task force was diverse in terms of company position, race, age, religion, gender, cultural background, and sexual orientation.

The task force produced the Strategic Diversity Plan, which was then individualized by each business unit. The individual plans included mentoring, rotational and special assignments, preparing competency models for management positions, strengthening the employee career planning process, conducting and analyzing exit interviews, and adding a diversity component to orientation and manager training. The company measured the progress of each business unit on a monthly basis, with the bonus of each unit head affected by the unit's year-end diversity results rating.

Pitney Bowes attributes part of the success of the strategy to open communication, accomplished through a newsletter and a video and within divisional communications meetings. Because of the plan, the number of women in management at Pitney Bowes increased steadily, reaching 16 percent of unit heads, vice presidents, executive directors, and directors by the time of the Catalyst Award. The company affirmed that developing and maintaining a diverse workforce is an essential business practice.

1995: Deloitte & Touche

Initiative for the Retention and Advancement of Women

The Initiative for the Retention and Advancement of Women of Deloitte & Touche, one of the nation's largest accounting and consulting firms, was created to develop, retain, and advance high-talent female professionals.

The first step toward change for Deloitte & Touche was the formation of a task force chaired by Chairman and CEO J. Michael Cook. The task force's recommendations led to the formation of the Council on the Advancement of Women—an external advisory group—to challenge the firm and keep it on track in meeting its goals.

The resulting initiative focused on changing the environment for women by enhancing career opportunities and supporting the balance of multiple commitments, an innovative approach in a client-driven environment. Components included "Men and Women as Colleagues," a two-day workshop on men and women working together; assignment reviews and career planning for women; accountability for the initiative's success at the office level; and internal communications such as videos and newsletters.

The initiative led to a drop in the turnover of women at all levels. At the senior manager level it dropped a significant 10 percent in two years, thereby eliminating the turnover differential between women and men at this key stage in their careers. In 1994, 18 percent of new partners were women.

1995: The Dow Chemical Company

Blueprint for Diversity

In the late 1980s, the Dow Chemical Company recognized diversity of its workforce as critical to its competitiveness. Accordingly, the company integrated its innovative diversity initiative into the company's strategic plan.

Dow created the Diversity Steering Team, made up of senior managers along with two advisory committees, to consider issues and make recommendations to the operating board. The Blueprint for Diversity included a system of measuring progress, making line management accountable for the hiring, retention, and advancement of women and people of color. It also included the tracking of high-potential women, career succession planning, training to increase manager sensitivity to diversity issues and to increase the ability of women and people of color to manage visibility and advancement, relocation assistance for dual-career couples, family care programs, and communication.

In a technology-based industry where women have found advancement difficult, Dow's initiative showed results. As of March 1995, the number of women in supervisory and management positions had doubled since 1989, and women made up 21 percent of Dow's workforce.

1995: J.C. Penney Company, Inc.

Fresh Perspective

The Catalyst Award–winning initiative of J.C. Penney Company, the nation's fourth-largest retailer, consisted of a comprehensive plan that included both internal programs and external events. At the center of the initiative was the Women's Advisory Team, nineteen women and men from all levels of management who worked with the Human Resources department and senior management to identify issues and foster the development of women. The team, backed up by local women's Advisory Teams at the company's many operating sites, helped the development of the company's career pathing system by creating a grid comparing all jobs by level, skills required, and steps in reaching the position. The grid clarified job opportunities, offering an effective way to deal with one of the major obstacles to women's advancement. As one key to success, the initiative included a system holding management accountable for women's advancement. Other elements included extensive diversity training and sponsorship of large, highly visible external events, such as the Juanita Kreps Award, the Race for the Cure, and women's leadership conferences.

As of March 1995, a woman headed one of J.C. Penney's four merchandise divisions, a $4 billion business in itself, and women held 21 percent of store district manager positions, 31 percent of regional business planning manager positions, and 13 percent of senior manager positions overall.

1996: Hoechst Celanese Corporation

Vertical Parity Initiative

Hoechst Celanese Corporation created its Vertical Parity Initiative in response to 1992 projections on the changing demographics of the workforce. The company inaugurated a method of measuring the progress of female and minority employees and making line managers—including middle management—accountable by linking 25 percent of bonuses to the achievement of diversity goals; an operating committee of senior managers monitored their performance in this area. Other aspects of the initiative included early identification of women with potential, mentoring, and a succession-planning program with tools for individual career design.

The initiative was named the "Vertical Parity Initiative" because of its goal of representing women and people of color at all levels in numbers mirroring the workforce from which the company recruited. By definition, it was woven into the fabric of the organization. It had specific five- and ten-year goals.

The initiative yielded measurable results—from 1991 to 1995 the number of women in senior management increased 20 percent.

1996: Knight-Ridder, Inc.

Strategic Career Development

In 1989, the Knight-Ridder Task Force on Diversity created a mandate to advance women and people of color that required all business units to develop numeric targets based on regional populations and to design programs to advance women to senior positions. This initiative—Strategic Career Development—included a management development review process in which vice presidents of Operations, News, and Human Resources conducted on-site reviews of career plans for high-potential employees.

The Executive Leadership Program for future publishers and heads of companies was key: 30 percent of participants were women. Companywide talent pools and mentoring programs ensured mobility across newspapers. And with goals that went beyond the company, newspapers conducted regular audits of bylines, photos, and experts to ascertain how women were represented and portrayed.

Women came to represent about 35 percent of executives and managers, a 12 percent increase from 1991; concurrently, a survey of women's readership of Knight-Ridder's newspapers showed a significant increase from 1991 to 1994.

1996: Texas Instruments

Teaming Up for Achievement

Texas Instruments found that breaking down its hierarchical structures by creating multilevel, cross-functional teams created opportunities for women by circumventing barriers that often obstructed women's careers. Such teams were the basis of the initiative Teaming Up for Achievement, in which an inclusive team environment brought increased visibility for women, access to key developmental assignments, and, in turn, advancement to senior management positions.

The *Dashboard*, a set of metrics that addressed the progress of women at all levels, facilitated measurement. The supportive corporate environment included a Women's Initiative Network, which offered leadership and mentoring opportunities at every site.

From the end of 1989 to 1995, the number of women with management, supervisory, or team leadership responsibilities increased nearly 50 percent.

1997: The Allstate Corporation

Creating an Environment for Success

Allstate moves the concept of corporate diversity forward into measurement and accountability with an on-line questionnaire called the Quarterly Leadership Measurement System, which all employees answer anonymously twice a year. Answers to such questions as "Does the company deliver quality service to customers regardless of ethnic background?" and "Does your immediate manager/team leader utilize different backgrounds and perspectives?" help the company create a Diversity Index from which to develop action plans and goals for annual improvement.

Rigorous succession planning includes identifying key positions nationwide (defined by importance to company strategy) and monitoring candidates by race, gender, and readiness; each appointment includes an affirmative action analysis and a measurement against diversity goals for each business.

Merit increases for managers are linked to achieving Diversity Index and succession planning goals. The initiative shows results: 40 percent of succession planning candidates are women and nearly half of senior- and executive-level women are in line positions. Also, as of December 1996, 19 percent of Allstate officers were women, up from 16 percent in 1993.

1997: Avon Mexico

Living a Vision for Women

A model for international operations, Avon Mexico not only stresses creating career opportunities for women and a culture where women can be successful, but also supports a broad range of women's interests in Mexico, including breast cancer research and women's athletics, academic scholarships, and cultural activities.

Underlying these efforts is the commitment of the top leaders of Avon Mexico, and of Avon Products, to be the company that "best understands and satisfies the product, service, and self-fulfillment needs of women globally." Avon Mexico participates in an annual executive resources review at Avon headquarters in New York where Avon's top brass identify the executives with the highest potential for development and advancement.

In a country where women make up only 20 percent of the workforce, Avon Mexico stands out, with women making up 54 percent of employees and 31 percent of managers within three reports of the president, up from 24 percent in 1993. Women now represent 38 percent of employees assigned to strategic task forces and the company pays particular attention to staffing teams with both women and men. Avon Mexico's vice president for sales was Mexico's first woman vice president; she is still one of only a few in the country.

1999 Catalyst Award
Application Guidelines:
What We Need From You

The 1999 Catalyst Award Evaluation Committee welcomes your nomination for the Catalyst Award. We will review nominations from corporations and professional firms on the following criteria: accountability, effective communication of initiative-based integration with business strategy and other programs, measurable results, originality, replicability, supportive environment, top management support, and senior-level leadership.

We encourage a range of initiatives or programs to apply. They do not need to have been designed exclusively for women but you must demonstrate the advancement benefits for women.

Part I. Initiative Summary

Your response to Part I should describe the initiative's key components and should answer the questions below in the form of a six- to eight-page summary. The Committee will also accept other supporting materials.

A. Business Rationale

- What was the business rationale that motivated this initiative?

- How has the business rationale been communicated to management and employees?

B. Target Population

- Who is targeted to benefit from this initiative?

- Does this initiative address issues that are specific to women of color?

C. Leadership

- Who are the key leaders of this initiative and what are their roles?

- How does key leadership communicate its commitment to this initiative?

D. Accountability

- How are managers educated about this initiative and held accountable for results?

- How are results monitored?

E. Supportive Environment

- In what ways does the corporate culture support women's advancement?

Part II

Describe the size of your workforce and the impact of the initiative within it. Cover at least the following points, and provide any other information that seems relevant.

- Please submit general workforce statistics, reflecting total numbers, not percentages, for women's executive and managerial positions at your organization and for executive and managerial women of color.

- Please provide data and statistics that indicate the impact of this initiative or program on the company, women overall, and women of color (e.g., turnover, recruitment, promotions, women on key assignments and in career development programs).

About Catalyst

Catalyst is a nonprofit organization with the mission of furthering women's advancement in corporations and professional firms. Catalyst studies this issue and advises chief executives, managers, and senior partners on how to capitalize on women's talent. Catalyst's Corporate Board Placement works with corporations recruiting women directors. The Catalyst Award annually recognizes corporate or professional initiatives promoting women's leadership. The organization's nationwide research on women in the workplace supports the hands-on work with corporations and firms–many of them each year—and what is learned out in the field enriches the research.

Founded in 1962, Catalyst anticipated that by century's end, gender would no longer be a factor in the workplace. But it has recently documented the status of women in corporate America and found that gender is not only still a factor, it largely determines career experiences. The 1996 Catalyst study *Women in Corporate Leadership: Progress and Prospects* surveyed Fortune 1000 CEOs and top women and found that the women were more than twice as likely as the CEOs to consider factors in the work environment—in the culture of the job itself—as barriers to advancement. The same survey showed a majority of responding Fortune 1000 CEOs to be ready to make changes to bring women into the highest ranks.

Catalyst annually counts the number of women among corporate board members, top earners, corporate officers, and senior managers in Fortune 500 companies, because in America, we measure what we value. Catalyst, with the encouragement and support of corporate leaders of both genders, provides accurate numbers—benchmarks, baselines, and headcounts—so that corporate leaders, numbers-driven, will make change for women at their organizations.

The annual *Catalyst Census of Women Directors of the Fortune 500* has shown an increase since counting began in 1993, probably in no small part because of the counting. In 1996, Catalyst began an annual *Census of Women Corporate Officers and Top Earners* that quantifies women's presence in the roles at the apex of American business. It documents just how many women hold important and influential positions in Fortune 500 companies, offering baseline data by which companies can judge future progress for women in corporate America.

Catalyst continues its cutting-edge research on such issues as work-family balance, women of color in corporate leadership, dual-career couples, and women entrepreneurs. Catalyst experts continue to diagnose workplace environments and help companies and firms develop strategies to enhance women's advancement and implement workable solutions. And Catalyst continues to count and to let America's leaders know where women are at their own companies and at those of their peers, because the competition out there grows steep, because the globe grows small, because America can no longer afford to waste its resources. Catalyst knows that what gets measured gets done.

CATALYST
120 Wall Street
New York, New York 10005-3904
212-514-7600
info@catalystwomen.org

Company Name Index

Subject Index

Industry Index

Best Practices Index